TO CHOOSE OUR FUTURE

AF731517

Development Alternatives

ACKNOWLEDGEMENT

'To Choose Our Future' presents the philosophy of the Development Alternatives (DA) Group, evolved from lessons learnt over the last three decades, to create a sustainable future for India. Today, India is at the crossroads on its path to improving the wellbeing of its citizens. Our nation must find the right balance between the imperatives of the here and now and the responsibilities for what we bequeath to future generations. Our children look to us to make the right choices now.

Standing on the shoulders of giants, we are trying to see further and understand deeper. Our journey so far has gained much from associations and friendships with the many who have shared our concerns and dreams for our nation and the world at large.

The DA Group would like to acknowledge communities in the hundreds of villages we have worked with across the country and especially those in Bundelkhand, who have allowed us to enter their lives so generously and permitted us to test our ideas, however unfamiliar or wild.

We also thank our many partners and collaborators whose work we have learnt from and built upon. We cannot forget the trust reposed in us by our many funders, both in India and outside, who have invested in our capacities and believe in our dreams. We would specially like to thank Heinrich Boell Stiftung whose encouragement and support inspired us to put together DA's philosophy for the future of our country on paper, which has resulted in this book.

We extend our special thanks to Rupinder Kaur (Renee) at Daalcheeni for her patience in putting our ideas to design so effectively. Thanks are due also to Sanu Kapila and his team at the Academic Foundation for publishing this work enabling its outreach. We would also like to thank the authorship of Freepik on flaticons.com and other 'Creative Commons' platforms who have so generously made their work and ideas available to be used in the book. In the same spirit, the book is licensed under Creative Commons to be shared with all for the design of a sustainable future for India and the world.

Not least, we are most in debt to the more than a thousand colleagues who have been a part of the Development Alternatives team at one time or another over the past three decades. It is their hard work on the ground and their sharp thinking in the analysis that constitutes the basis of this presentation.

TO CHOOSE **OUR FUTURE**

With the departure of its colonial rulers in 1947, India regained the opportunity to choose a completely new future for herself. What was unique in this opportunity was not just the ability to build a new nation drawing on the best features of her enormously rich cultural and civilisational traditions, (and to discard those that were not acceptable for the welfare of ALL its citizens), but to mesh these with the extraordinary new understanding of our world generated by science over the last century.

Unfortunately, within three decades following independence, it had become clear that the opportunity had been wasted and our new nation had lost its way, much less fulfilled its role as a model for others. By the early 1980s, when Development Alternatives was set up, the brightest young people in India who had the means to do so, were abandoning their country in droves and trans-locating as far away as possible to improve their life prospects. The nation's economy and society were close to breakdown with poverty, corruption, and mal-governance as reality and a dominant self-image of the country. A decade later, in the early 1990s, substantial economic reforms were introduced to rescue the nation's economy, which was close to bankruptcy. These gave immediate relief to the national exchequer and, to some extent the national psyche. However, it also laid the framework of a rapid transition from a dysfunctional 'socialist' economy to a predatory 'neoliberal' economy – and as the number of millionaires grew, so did the numbers of the hungry and deprived.

'To Choose Our Future' is an attempt to summarise some of the lessons learned by Development Alternatives from recent Indian history and its 30-year journey through India, analysing what went wrong in these transitions and how they can be put right for the future. Its perspective is universal and the aim is to identify the changes needed to make India a home for all - the poor, the well-off and the future generations. It tries to suggest ways by which a more sustainable balance can be achieved among different segments of society and between society and the natural ecosystems. The book presents a reasoned case for substantial changes in national priorities as a means of bringing the future trajectory of India's economy in line with its social aspirations and the limits of its environmental resources.

contents

VISION: THE FUTURE WE WANT

Where the mind is without fear and the head is held high

Where knowledge is free

Where the world has not been broken up into fragments

By narrow domestic walls

Where words come out from the depth of truth

Where tireless striving stretches its arms towards perfection

Where the clear stream of reason has not lost its way

Into the dreary desert sand of dead habit

Where the mind is led forward by thee

Into ever-widening thought and action

Into that heaven of freedom, my Father, let my country awake."

- Rabindranath Tagore, 1910 (Bengali) 1930 (English)

These words of national ambition, though they were penned more than a century ago representing an anguished *cri de coeur* of a country quashed for generations under colonial rule, sadly remain true for the great majority of Indians today.

Much has undeniably been achieved in our country since its tryst with destiny. The lives of hundreds of millions of our fellow citizens continue to get gradually and measurably better with the passing of each year. Many of us live longer and have opportunities not inferior to those who live in the most advanced economies. Yet, even more hundreds of millions still await entry into "that heaven of freedom" – where there is freedom from hunger, deprivation and want, and from ignorance and fear – which we all desire and deserve. While much has been achieved, so much more remains to be done for an India as it can be, of what it should be: an India of our collective dreams, aspirations and endeavours.

65 years of being an independent Republic, the fundamental question that remains is whether the poet's aspirations will be fulfilled, not just for a few but for all our compatriots within a reasonable time horizon. Would it be too much to ask whether - by 2047 when India celebrates her hundredth anniversary - every citizen can happily say, "the mind is without fear and the head is held high"?

We envision such an India, truly free, where all citizens enjoy the health, dignity, and fulfilment to which they are entitled. A nation where everyone has access to at least the products and services that meet his or her basic needs – adequate nutrition, water, sanitation, shelter, clothing, education, health care, mobility, livelihood opportunity, personal security and vibrant community life.

We aspire to a nation that recognises the essential need for diversity in all aspects of life - biological, socio-cultural, technological, economic and physical - to nurture a sustainable society. Its institutions would translate this commitment into policies and actions that reconcile the imperatives of universality while ensuring wellbeing, peace and social harmony. This India ensures all citizens have equal opportunities to lead lives of dignity and to participate meaningfully in their community, which implies that they see their society as fair and just; and all economic activity is geared to satisfying the basic needs of all while recognising the limits of the natural resource endowment and the environment.

Our India would be a land where every citizen has a real, tangible opportunity to build a future of his or her choice and to contribute to building a strong and resilient nation. Our economy would be driven by the need to achieve universal human fulfilment and happiness rather than by the pursuit of economic indicators such as GDP, FDI and Sensex, which are simply numbers representing financial transactions that reflect a very limited aspect of the nation's economy. These would be replaced by indicators that reflect true wellbeing of individuals and society. The systems of governance would support policies and actions for a truly resilient and sustainable future for India. The economic policies would, by intention and design, conserve and restore ecosystems and the natural processes that support it. Ours would be a nation where people have a sense of ownership and responsibility for all their resources and act as guardians to prevent activities those are against the interest of the nation's peace and security.

Modern India, perhaps more than any other society, has a lineage of dedication to living in harmony with nature as witnessed the teachings of the Vedas, Mahavir, the Buddha and Guru Nanak. Inspired by this social and cultural heritage, this India adopts and showcases lifestyles and livelihoods that could bring our planet back from the brink of destruction. It is committed to the values of fairness, equity justice that converge integrally and inextricably in the lives and ideals of the founders of our Republic, most distinctly demonstrated by Mahatma Gandhi's steadfast and non-negotiable dedication to the values of *Antodaya* (putting the last first) and *Ahimsa* (non-voilence): going so far as to put the last person first and mother nature at the centre of all individual and societal concern.

THE NEED FOR ALTERNATIVES IN DEVELOPMENT

To make the India we envision a reality, we must assess where our systems of governance, industry, education and behaviour are leading us.

Will the marginalised be able to walk with pride and dignity on that journey?

Are the pathways leading us to the top of the plateau or down the precipice?

Will we all have enough to eat and drink or will some plunder and loot and damage the ladder for the rest?

Will our economic vehicle be driven on wheels of equity; human capacity, nature's bounty and human enterprise, fuelled by green investments to accommodate all, and at a pace that helps us reach our destination?

We would like to think that this destination is real, very real, and possible to reach. We have to replace our engines and change the road we choose. It will, however, not be so simple. The change may require changing of the drivers - fundamental transformations in our institutional structures, behaviour patterns, ideologies and indeed value systems. We need a collective approach to define a new, transformative and universal new development agenda for the country. This requires the galvanisation of national political will such that each citizen can play a role according to his or her capacity and relevant to the context for a fair and just transformation.

We need to refashion our institutional systems and transform our current attitudes to virtually all aspects of society and the economy - consumption patterns and wellbeing, technology and production systems, enterprise and distributive justice - all of which have in the light of today's circumstances and knowledge need to be reoriented to conform to the principles of an inclusive and circular economy. This implies that the poorest and marginalised are put at the centre of economic and social attention and the restoration and regeneration natural systems become the boundary conditions that must not be transgressed, not just for future generations but also for those of today.

Such a transformation will require us to shift the direction of our investments towards building human capacity, especially focusing on women, youth and the marginalised; creating local institutions and infrastructure; and regenerating our natural wealth. We will need substantial investments in cross-cutting innovations in technology, institutions and production systems as means to achieve these desired outcomes. It will also require some to cut back on over-consumption so that those who do not have enough get the space to achieve fulfilment of their basic needs, actualise their potential and live in a safe and secure world.

The future lies elsewhere and in alternative approaches. India can only become a vibrant, prosperous democracy if it stops imitating the West (much of which is itself now facing very serious economic and ecological crises). This means that we must now get off the bandwagon of neoliberal economics and adopt societal and economic visions more appropriate for India. For example, we need to adopt a more suitable mix of scales, from the big and centralised where needed and the small and local where possible (for institutions of governance, education, business and civil society); and embrace consumption patterns and production systems that are resource efficient and to minimise material waste and provide enough for all.

Development Alternatives was set up three decades ago to address such issues to pioneer change for such a future for India. It was set up to develop alternative approaches and solutions to these problems that are now known to all.

We at Development Alternatives, are dreamers and we dream BIG with our eyes open, our feet firmly on the ground, our arms stretched wide to receive new ideas and our head held high with dignity of lives well led. Our lens has been ground with the powder of compassion and commitment to a fair society and polished with the cloth of oneness with nature - which we see as the essence of our India and the basis of human survival. We believe in simple ideals for complex societies: thinking holistically and designing systemically rather than the current resort to narrow, sectoral, silo-based approaches for decision-making; working strategically and finding the right balance between the hit-and-run profits of the immediate and the large gains possible in the long term; and a much greater commitment than in the past to a future that is secure, fulfilling and sustainable for all.

Therefore, in the true spirit of dreamers we design the India we feel that our children and theirs will be proud to live in but as *karmayogis* we act in partnership with whoever will join us to make this dream come true.

01

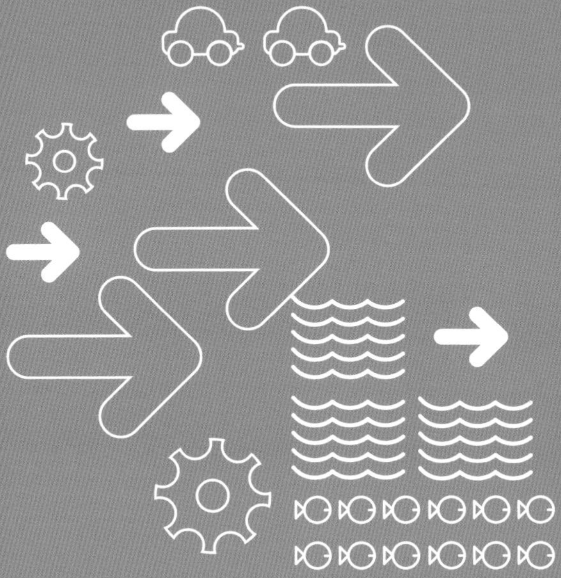

OUR GUIDING *Principles*

The Panchsheel of Development Alternatives

- Principle of Universality
- Principle of System Integrity
- Principle of Efficiency
- Principle of Sufficiency
- Principle of Harmony

OUR GUIDING PRINCIPLES

The Panchsheel of Development Alternatives

The successive changes in political and economic ideology in India have led to constantly changing development agendas and priorities for the last six decades.

We present at the start of the book five principles - 'The *Panchsheel*[1] of Development Alternatives' , which we believe must be satisfied by all policies and interventions that are intended to create a sustainable future for India.

In our usage, a 'principle' is a fundamental truth or proposition that serves as the foundation for a system of belief or behaviour or for a chain of reasoning. These five guiding principles have been developed from the learning and experiences of Development Alternatives in its thirty years of work - from the literature and from engagement with our local, regional and global partners. Our effort is to stay as true as we can to these principles in all our work and be guided by them in making our contributions to the sustainable economic, social and environmental development of our nation.

Principle of Universality

Fairness and social justice are bedrock values in all faiths and traditions. Mahatma Gandhi's talisman, which is another way of expressing his concepts of 'antodaya' or 'putting the last first', is an apt description of the ethical basis of a well-functioning, decent, and sustainable society. Commitment to universality implies inclusion and empowerment of all, particularly those who are marginalised and voiceless. It entails an equitable distribution of economic and natural wealth, and an opportunity for all its citizens to pursue better lives and participate in decisions that affect their lives.

Equity and justice are not simply moral issues: they are a practical societal requirement – a prerequisite for civilisational survival. No society can be good for long - for either the rich or the poor - if the most deprived and marginalised are not living with dignity and fulfilment. An equitable, participatory and a just society is essential for economic progress and vital for the health of the ecological system that supports it.

Principle of System Integrity

The principle of system integrity is based on the concept of 'the whole is greater than the sum of its parts'. A critical element of this principle is the requirement to understand how parts of the system influence one another within the whole and how the relationship of the whole weighs on the parts. Even though problems of poverty, inequality, jobless growth are all inter-linked and demand a systemic, holistic, and a coordinated approach, policy instruments often adopt a disjointed perspective to achieve results, ignoring the interdependencies amongst systems, sectors and scales.

Given the many dots that need to be connected in the process of amalgamating socio, economic and environment development, sustainable development can best be achieved using a synergistic approach. By understanding the underlying structure and relationships, we can better identify how development interventions ripple through the whole system and recognise under what circumstances the interaction of elements of the system would behave differently. Such an approach provides a holistic understanding of trade-offs thereby maximising productivity, efficiency and other gains manifold while minimising unintended consequences. This principle highlights the value of integration and interconnections, emphasising coherence and coordination among various policies and actions for development.

Principle of Efficiency

The principle of efficiency means to get more from less. It means reducing the rate of use of resources for the same output and also raising output while reducing negative environmental impacts. To bring about a balance between the ever-expanding demands of human economy and the declining productive capacity of nature's ecological systems will require an increase in resource productivity and eco-efficiency.

The principle helps alleviate the problem of scarcity and responds to the sustainability challenge of intergenerational equity by reducing the rate of physical resource depletion, while simultaneously helping to reduce costs by raising resource productivity. Raising efficiency involves sophisticated knowledge of technological and psycho-social systems. It implies using resources better, more wisely and more cleanly to maximise productivity.

Principle of Sufficiency

The excessive demands and over-consuming lifestyles of the wealthier segments of society are placing immense stress on the environment while the poor, on the other hand, are unable to meet their very basic needs such as food, health care, shelter and education. The principle of sufficiency requires a change in people's lifestyles and mind-sets promoting the belief for those who use too many resources that less can be better. Such a transition would enable those who need more material resources for a decent life can have access to them, without society, overall, transgressing planetary boundaries.

Sufficiency will necessitate the rich to cut their use of the rapidly depleting resources of the planet to ensure wellbeing for all. They will need to speedily cap their resource consumption and work towards a life of sufficiency. For the poor, the process will be a bit more complicated and slower as they will need access to more resources until they have reached an acceptable level of consumption, which might be termed sufficient. After which they, too, will have to control their use of natural resources. Improvement in life prospects of the poor provides a double benefit for all insofar as this is the parameter that most effectively reduces the size of families and the rate of growth of population.

Principle of Harmony

The principle of harmony underscores the imperative for a civilization to fulfil the needs and aspirations of the current generation while maintaining the productivity of nature to provide for an even better future to the subsequent ones. It implies harmonious co-existence among the very diverse fabrics of our economic organisations, societal structures and natural systems and is the key to a sustainable future for humankind.

The diversity of our socio-economic and natural systems is the basis on which humanity and civilization have the adaptability to organise themselves and evolve over time. To cope with the exigencies of an uncertain and constantly changing world, communities and societies need to acquire resilience, which comes with systems (technological, institutional and natural) that are flexible, capable of learning and adapting. Multifunctional systems, based on small, decentralised, self-organising sub-systems with governance at each level tailored to the needs of that level often offer the most effective and resilient solutions to today's world.

Moreover, there exists an obvious relationship between the diversity of natural systems and the diversity, health and sustainability of human systems - cultural, social and economic. For both ethical and practical reasons, no human action should jeopardise the continued existence and health of any form of life, particularly biodiversity and ecosystems.

02

THE PRESENT

We Have

India...Pulling together or pushing apart?

- Where did we go wrong?
- So, where are we now?
- Do We Need a New Development Model ?

A **PROGRESSING** INDIA!

PERCENTAGE OF POPULATION IN POVERTY

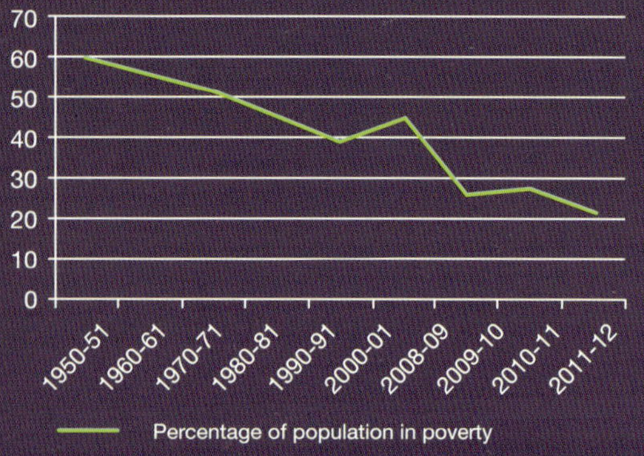

INDEX OF INDUSTRIAL PRODUCTION

(2004-05=100)

FOODGRAIN OUTPUT

[in million tonnes]

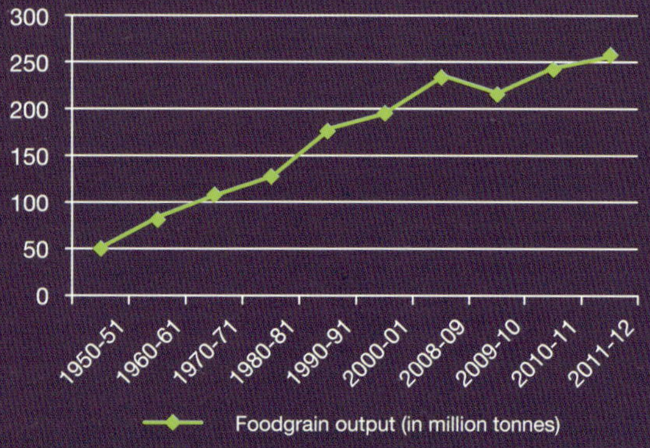

ELECTRICITY GENERATED [utilities only]

[billion KWH]

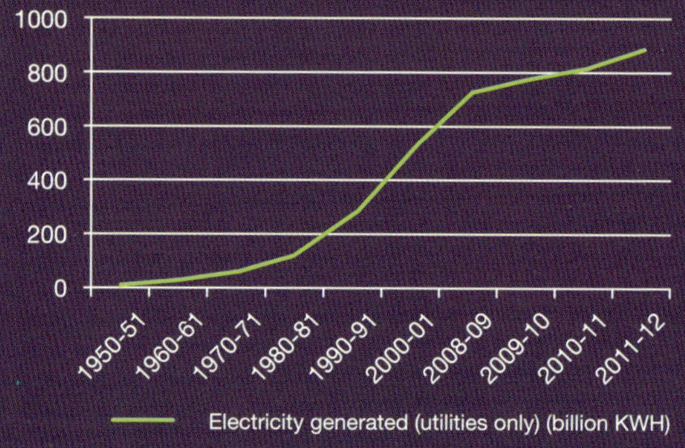

Source: Based on data from NSSO, Economic Survey of India & Planning Commission, 2012

THE PRESENT WE HAVE

India...pulling together or pushing apart?

Over the past six decades, India as a whole has made undeniable, and often quite dramatic, progress on many fronts. People have attained unprecedented levels of health, wealth, and knowledge.

Food production has grown to levels inconceivable even a few decades ago. An ever-growing range of products from industry is accessible to an ever-growing range of customers. Cheap sources of energy have made possible facilities for travel and communication that enable large numbers of people to live a life of convenience and comfort on a scale never known before. Many diseases have been largely eliminated, and life expectancy has risen significantly. And, the proportion of the population living in extreme poverty declined rapidly from an approximated 65 per cent[2] in the 1950s to 22 per cent[3] today.

India's achievements in industry, agriculture, and space science are well known with her young professionals and entrepreneurs competing with the best worldwide. Some of the world's largest IT companies, banks, airlines, and other businesses are run by Indian CEOs; as are large Indian multinational corporations, some of which own iconic global brands such as Jaguar Cars and Corus Steel.

Since 1991, India has created more than 100 billionaires, becoming the third ranking country in this field, who are supported by some 150,000 millionaires, many of them newly minted.[4]

India has made extraordinary strides in building up a vast modern economy in a very short time frame, much shorter than the one taken by the nations of Europe and North America who modernised earlier at a more leisurely pace and when financial capital was cheap and plentiful. India has made transitions in industry, infrastructure, agriculture, and other sectors in the last two decades that took the industrialised countries nearly two centuries to achieve.

Many of us now have more, control more and know more than ever before.

Yet, the overall picture of our economy is not as healthy as these facts might suggest. Owing to the fast pace and process of development, it is only natural to expect some strains and tensions in the economic structures built at top speed by India. New and emerging concerns such as widespread lack of purchasing power, ecosystem degradation, climate change, materials scarcity, and the demand for resources that exceeds what nature can supply are hindering our country's ability to grow as others did. The unprecedented creation of wealth among a few is going hand in hand with unheard-of expansion of poverty for the many, loss of societal resilience, destruction of the environmental resource base, erosion of political democracy and rampant unemployment. This dichotomy is cause for deep worry about the efficacy of the development model and trajectory we have chosen.

These factors raise certain pertinent questions such as:

- ***Can the current neoliberal policies deliver a viable, sustainable future for India?***
- ***Can we expect the 'Trickle-Down' ever to work within a reasonable time frame?***
- ***What do we have to do to get on to the road to a sustainable future?***

Such questions may sound simple, but they go to the heart of the rather complex reality we find ourselves in. Political, academic, and public discourses have not adequately addressed these kinds of queries with those who champion either extreme of the political spectrum - straight socialism on the one hand and capitalism on the other. The pendulum swing from one end to the other has retarded, in different ways at each end, the development of our economy for more than sixty-five years. Unfortunately no matter what political ideology is in power at any time, neither the economy nor the society have been very secure.

Where did we go wrong?

For the first forty years of its nationhood, India suffered from a mismanaged 'socialist' economy in which the roles of government and business were badly mixed up. The government was running power stations, steel mills, pharmaceutical companies, airlines, hotels, and parts of every other sector of the economy. It was so busy managing businesses that it could hardly fulfil its mandate as the guardian of the nation's policies, regulations, and enforcement mechanisms, let alone function as the enabler of creativity or enterprise. The private sector, on the other hand, was busy cultivating connections and running the government from behind the scenes. This crossover of responsibilities meant that the economy could neither generate the goods and services it needed nor the jobs and purchasing power that the consumers required. The winning role model that India was supposed to be for the global South in the 1950s, with its mixed economy, non-capitalist model of development and a welfare state, gradually lost out. Meanwhile other Asian economies such as Taiwan and Korea moved ahead because of their much clearer demarcation of responsibilities and careful nurturing of synergies between the public and private sector.

From this period, when the primary narrative (though not necessarily action) of pubic policy was about alleviating poverty (mostly through earmarked government 'schemes'), in 1991 India suddenly jumped into an era of stock market indexes, measures to raise FDI, deregulation and liberalisation of industry. The arrival of these neoliberal reforms flooded the Indian markets with monies creating opportunities for a few to become obscenely wealthy and stagnancy in real development for most of the rest. These 'reforms' abandoned parts of the socialist model and reliance on crony capitalism was raised to a much higher order, rapidly making a few rich people even richer and large numbers at the bottom of the pyramid poorer, some relatively and others absolutely.

However, the electoral implications of the demographic profile of India means that no matter how high the commitment to neoliberal policies, no government could remain in power for long without committing strong socialist inspired promises to provide welfare services and subsidies by the state, such as for employment generation, farm inputs, and food. Such promises whether delivered on or not, were often very costly, financially, psychologically and culturally. Since these 'reforms' were never fully implemented and had inbuilt contradictions, they have led us to jumbled results that could not slow down the growing economic disparity, increasing social alienation, and massive environmental destruction.

So, where are we now?
on our social progress...

India has come a long way on social progress since its Independence. The proportion of people living in extreme poverty has reduced from 65 percent of the population to 22 percent today. Our education systems have nurtured scholars that are contributing positively at the global level. Literacy levels have improved from a mere 18 percent since independence to 75 percent today.[5] We have access to world-class healthcare infrastructure and eradicated diseases like polio. Improvements in life expectancy (from 40 years to 60 years)[6] and fertility rates (from 5.8 to 2.5)[7] are all indicators that suggest improvement for an upward trajectory. India boasts a culture of entrepreneurship and innovation; pioneering the global IT services industry, and has a global diaspora of many outstanding academics, political leaders, businesspersons and civil society members around the globe.

While poverty, in terms of percentages has seen a rapid decline, the absolute number of poor, which is the number that really counts, has gone up from 200 million[8] in the 1950s to about 270 million[9] people today (and much higher by other estimates). And while many may have been pulled above the poverty line, there is still high vulnerability amongst our nouveau non-poor - three out of five of these are in high danger of being pushed back below the official poverty line with even a slight economic shock.[10]

As the largest liberal democracy in the world, while India has campaigned hard to position itself as a credible major player in the global economy, it is difficult to gain this credibility when the country has neglected to enable a large section of its people to get access to even their most basic needs – health, education, jobs, food or nutrition, shelter, energy, water, and sanitation. Ranking 102 out of 132 countries on the Social Progress Index[11] , and 135 out of 187 countries on the Human Development Index[12] in 2014, India homes one of the largest populations of poor and hungry persons. It also hosts the highest number of households without toilets or regular supply of electricity and the biggest set of communities that cannot offer even basic education or healthcare. Inadequate access to basic needs further reduces the capability of the poor to participate in the economic system, trapping them in a vicious cycle of poverty. The statistics for basic need

NO PLACE TO GO

THE WORST OFFENDERS IN INDIA'S GREAT TOILET TRICK

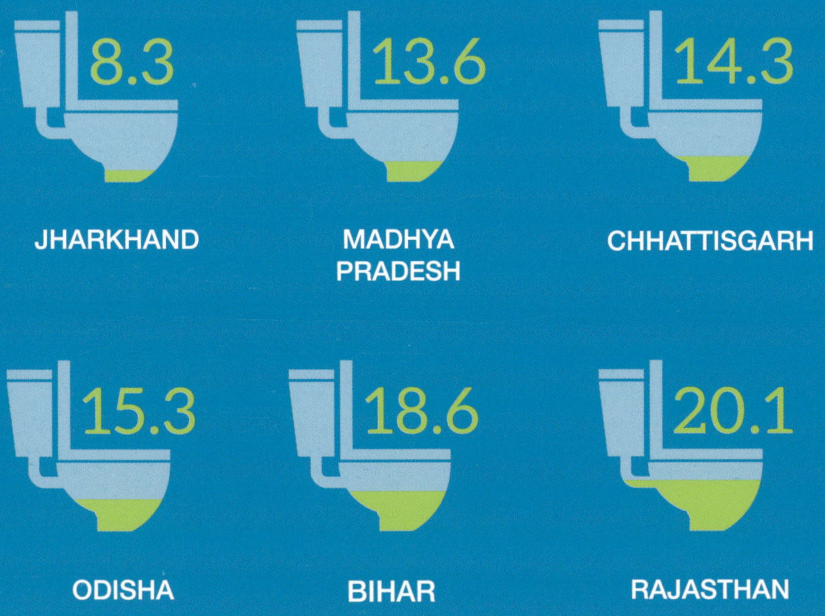

* Per cent Sanitation Coverage

Source: Based on the Census of India, 2011

626 million

in India practice open defecation

75%

of India's surface water resources are polluted

ENVIRONMENTAL

386,000

children under the age of five die each year in india from diarrhoea, through fecal-oral transmission

HUMAN HEALTH

120 million

a year from labor sick days, counting the cost of treatment and the loss of production

ECONOMIC

indicators reflect an appalling state, however these too seem to be odd with the reality as most of these are coverage statistics do not account for operating capacity, quality, functionality, adequacy, usage, equity of distribution, access and sustainability. This poverty trap results in low incomes, large families, and undernourished workers, which lead to a widespread inability to save or invest in building the skills needed to jump out and participate meaningfully in a modern economy.

Deprivation towards basic needs and opportunity is further compounded for the vulnerable and marginalised sections of society, especially women. The traditional patriarchal norms, not all of which have been set aside, have relegated women to secondary status creating a collection of disparate and interlinked problems in Indian society. Indicators reveal that in terms of education, access to economic opportunities, and overall health status, women fare worse than men. This drastically inhibits not only their

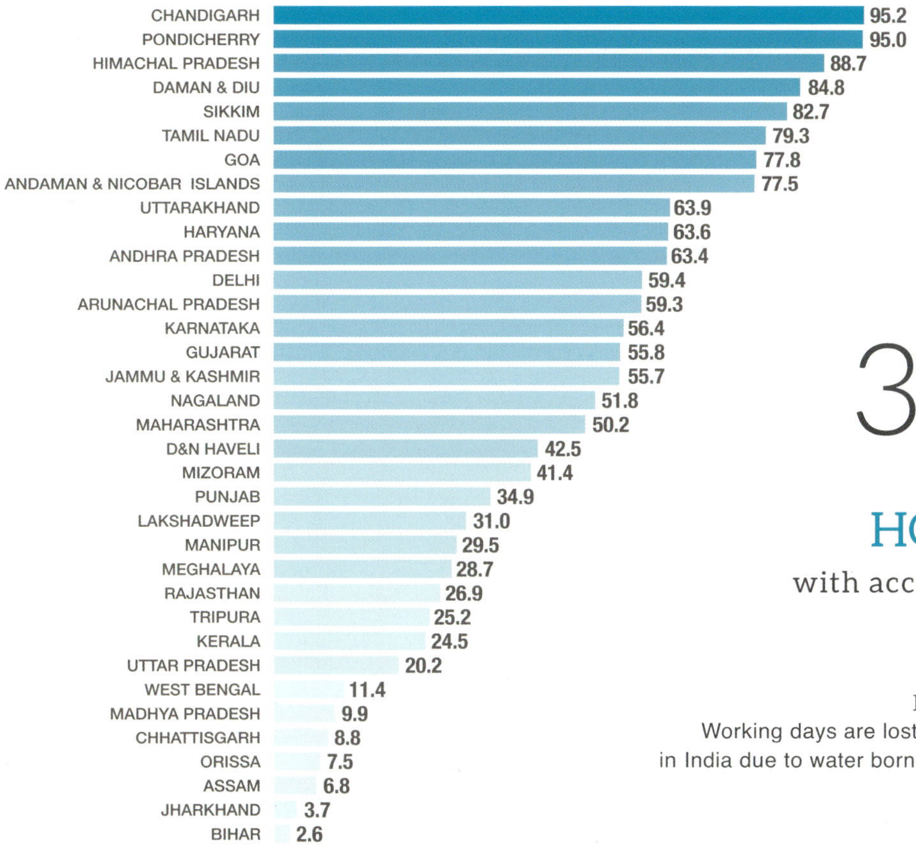

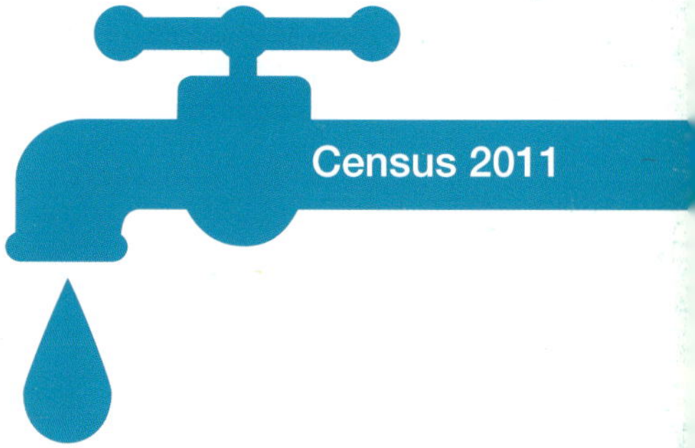

30.8%

RURAL

HOUSEHOLDS

with access to TAP WATER (in %)

73 million
Working days are lost each year in India due to water borne diseases
(PCI, 2012)

103.8 million
lack safe water
(water.org, 2013)

Source: Ministry of Drinking Water and Sanitation

HALF THE SKY IN DESPAIR

- WOMEN IN INDIA

1 in 3 malnourished

Every third woman in India is malnourished. Every second is anaemic.

(National Family Health Survey, 2006)

35.4% illiterate

women in India are illiterate as against 18% men.

(Census of India, 2011)

20% of 275 million

formal labour worksforce

Women constitute only 20% of the total formal labour workforce 275 million.

(Planning Commission, 2013)

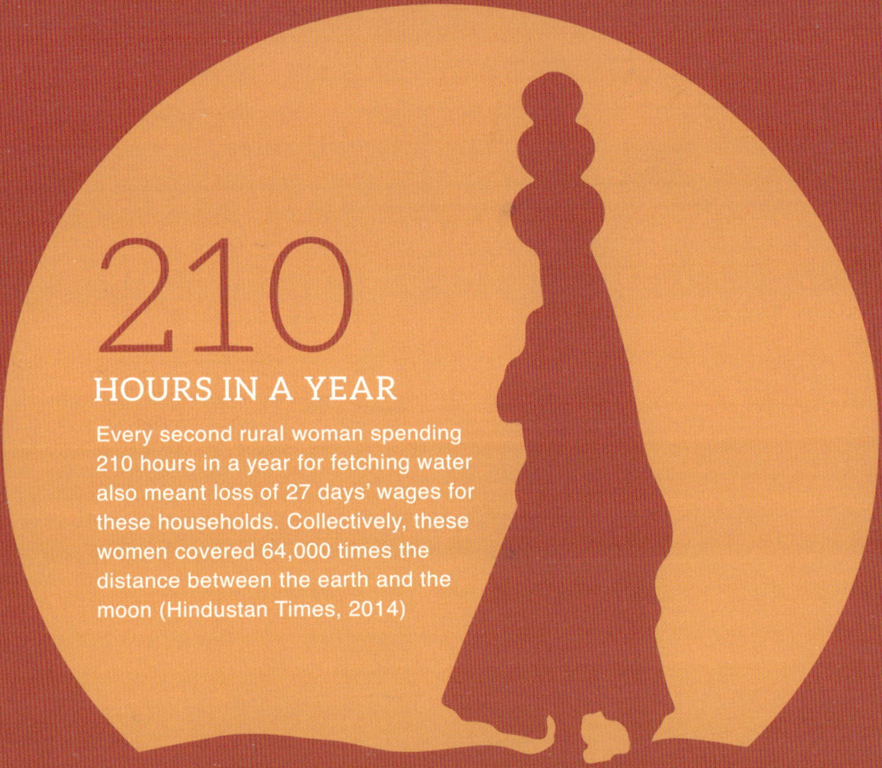

210 HOURS IN A YEAR

Every second rural woman spending 210 hours in a year for fetching water also meant loss of 27 days' wages for these households. Collectively, these women covered 64,000 times the distance between the earth and the moon (Hindustan Times, 2014)

11% of seats in

National Parliament

Women occupy only 11% seats in the Lower and Upper Houses of the National Parliament, a dismal figure when compared to the average of only 20%

(Inter Press Service, 2014)

abilities to deliver on their potential to improve decision making and participate in the socio-economic system but also adversely affects the development of their families and thus, the community as a whole.

Poverty and deprivation is a complex issue, deeply intertwined with economic, political, social, cultural, psychological, and environmental factors. The official poverty figure of the Planning Commission (Government of India), based on calorie intake, education, and health criteria, estimates those below the poverty line at 270 million in 2012-2013.[13] The equivalent figure for this measure in 2004-05 was estimated at 407.1 million[14] by the Planning Commission while the same government's National Commission for Enterprises in the Unorganised Sector using equally plausible criteria estimated it at 836 million[15] for the same year.

There are many other credible sources such as the United Nations, research institutes, universities, companies and the other official international bodies that estimate the number of poor using varied perspectives and

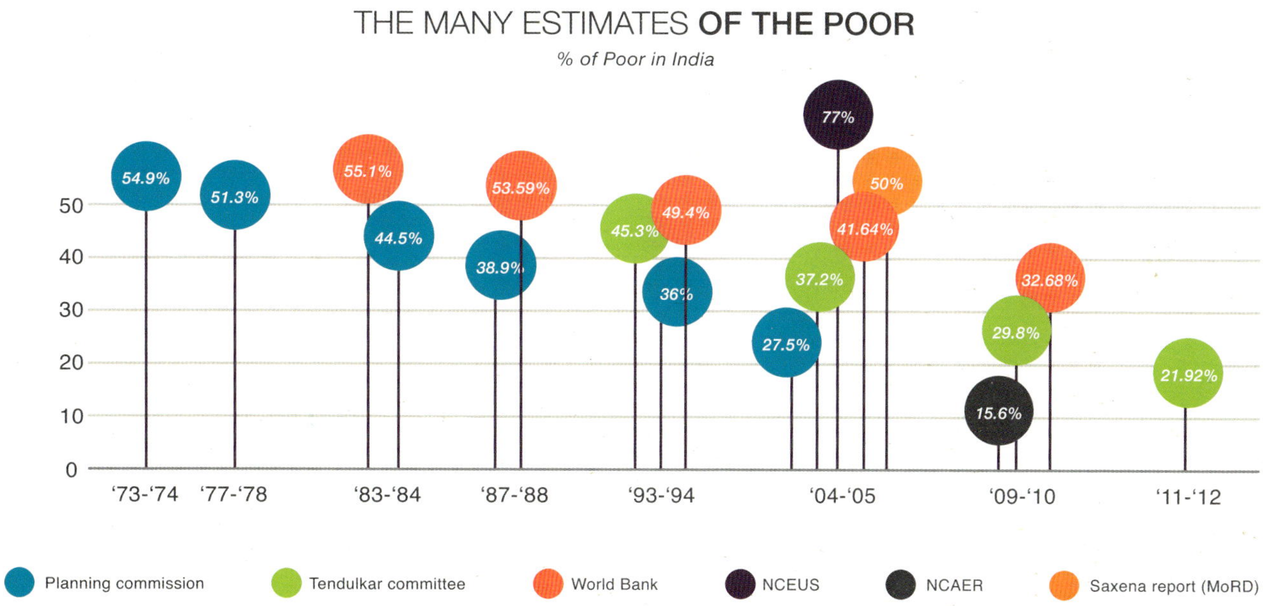

Over the years, there have been many estimates of the number of poor in this country. The most notable are those by the Planning Commission which counts to estimate 'how much' poverty, and the Ministry of Rural Development which identifies the poor to know 'who' is living below the poverty line. The varying definitions and approaches to count the poor have produced a range of estimates.

Adapted from: thealternative.in, 2013

The Empowerment Gap, at Rs. 332,000 crore ($69 billion), is seven times larger than the poverty gap

Average monthly consumption expenditure
INR per capita per month, 2011-12, in 2011-12

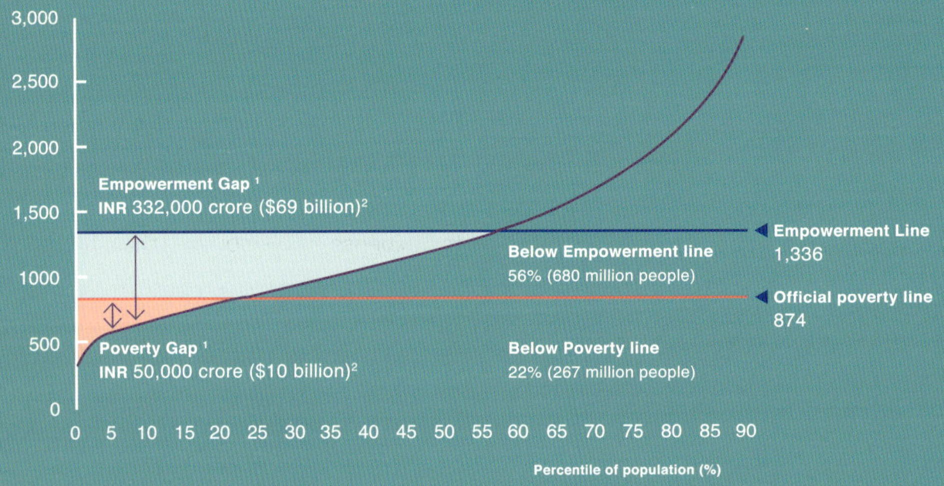

1. The Empowerment Gap and the poverty gap are defined as the aggregate differential between actual private consumption expenditure and the consumption requirements of the empowerment line and the poverty line, respectively.
2. Using average exchange rate of $1 = INR 48.0769 for April 2011 - March 2012

The Empowerment Line, developed by McKinsey Global Institute, is an analytical framework that determines the level of consumption required to fulfill eight basic needs—food, energy, housing, drinking water, sanitation, health care, education, and social security—at a level sufficient to achieve a decent standard of living rather than bare subsistence. In applying this metric to India in 2012, 56 percent of the population lacked the means to meet essential needs. By this measure, some 680 million Indians experienced deprivation, more than 2.5 times the population of 270 million below the official poverty line.The Empowerment Line diagram here shows that the additional consumption (the Empowerment Gap) needed to give 680 million people decent living standards is seven times higher than the cost of eliminating poverty as defined by the government.

Source: McKinsey Global Institute (2014)

methodologies. For instance, 640 million people are counted as poor according to more holistic measures of poverty such as the Multi-Dimensional Poverty Index of the Oxford University[16] while the Empowerment Gap of the McKinsey Global Institute states that 680 million[17] people are deprived of basic needs and amenities.

Despite the many estimates and details of arguably the single most important economic parameter from a national policy perspective, we have to wonder where we have failed to identify the problem and gone wrong in putting in place appropriate systems, measures and action to bring about change in the lives of the people of our country.

on our economic development...

With its spectacular take off in economic growth in the last two decades, India is now positioned as one of the fastest growing economies in the world. Playing an important role as a leader among the developing nations and recognised as a member of the BRICS group, India's economic progress has been significant. Total industrial output and productivity, size of foreign investments and share in international trade have seen unprecedented levels of growth since independence. India's food grain production has increased five fold over the decades that followed colonial rule to a record 260 million tonnes[18] in the fiscal year 2013. However, despite this credible progress, there are still more than 600 million people (double the entire population of India in 1947) who cannot access their basic needs.

Economic growth is, in reality, simply a means to achieve development - for our purpose defined as a pathway towards long-term wellbeing for people and the planet. Unfortunately, much of this "economic growth" we have made has been achieved at the expense of natural and social capital that have diminished precipitously as a result. This unprecedented creation of wealth has gone hand in hand with expansion of poverty and inequality accompanied by destruction of our forests, rivers and soils. What is becoming clearly evident is that the theories on which our current economic systems of production and distribution rest today - growth must come first, even at the expense of distributive injustice and human misery - efficiency over equity...machines over people....the rich before the poor...development over environment, will not work for very long.

Chasing GDP as the sole indicator of development has created a "series of fallacies, false assumptions and distortions" contrary to our "constitutional vision of '*Abhyudaya*', the humanist development".[19] In this GDP chase, the modern Indian economy is headed to an era where cheap machines produce even cheaper products for other cheap machines to use. As a consequence, human beings have less and less to do – and less and less to do it with. It is common to see more and more automation in the face of more unemployed people – followed by more and more products chasing less and less purchasing power. The labour saving technologies and mechanistic economic structures are leading to a growing supply and stagnant demand.[20]

This era of accelerated economic growth and globalisation is not creating jobs at the rate needed to keep up with the growth of the labour force resulting in growing income

THE RISE OF INFORMAL WORKERS

Number of Employees in the informal sector (in millions)

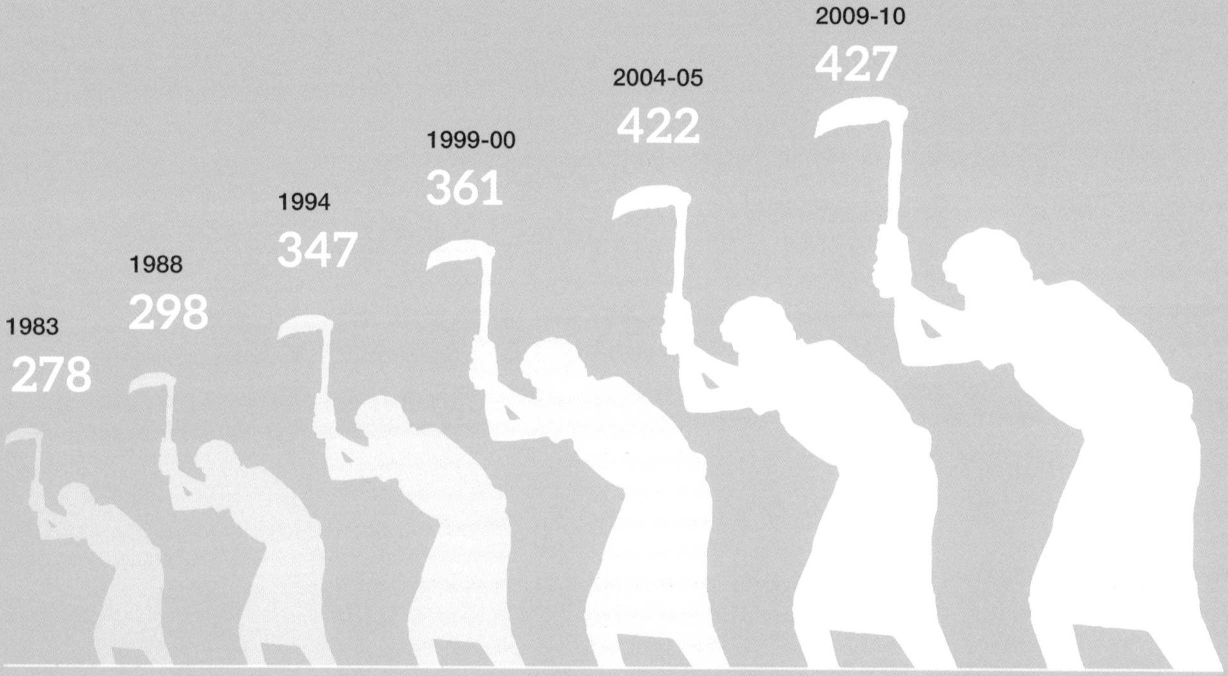

Sources: for 2009-10: computed from NSS 66th round, 2004-05 and 1999-00:NCEUS, 1983-1994: NSS rounds in Bairagya 2010

inequality. One of the most disturbing numbers to this effect is data from the National Sample Survey (2009-10) that shows addition of merely 2.76 million work opportunities in the high growth period five year period of 2005-2010 as compared to the addition of 60 million to the workforce during the period 1999-2005.[21] Among the many reasons for this decline is also a decrease in self-employment opportunities, which dropped by 25.5 million[22] because of the poor support available to entrepreneurs. Indeed, the indications are that certain kinds of jobs, including those in large industry and agriculture, are being lost and that there continues to be a net addition every year of several million people to the pool of the unemployed. The economy would be heading for a total disaster if it were not for the micro and small enterprises and the informal sector. Moreover, the 'skill gap' – disconnect between skills needed by employers and those that are available in the job market – is costing India dearly in terms of business

EMPLOYMENT
IN THE ORGANISED SECTOR

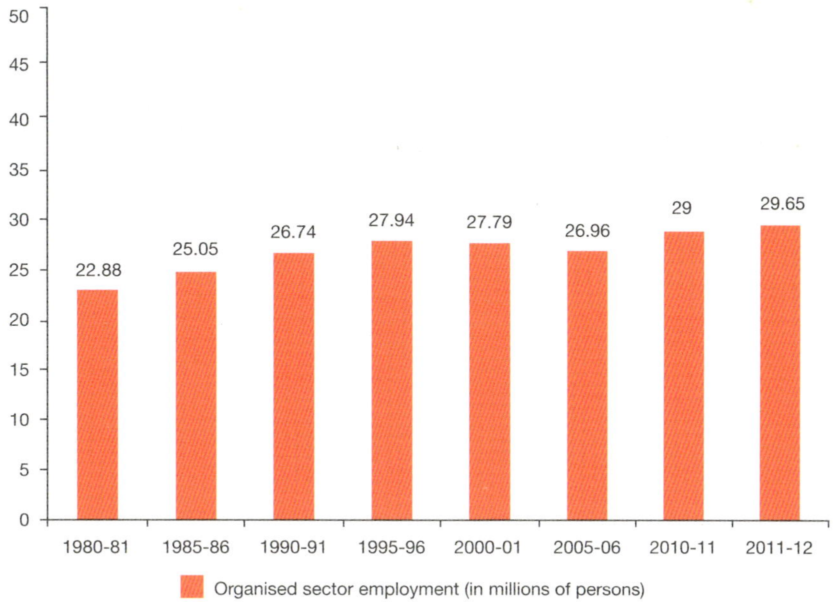

Source: Directorate General of Employment and Training, Ministry of Labour and Employment, Government of India, 2012

and employment. Our education and training systems have failed to evolve in response to the needs of the market, accentuating the problem of joblessness in the country.

The favouring of our economic policies for a privileged few, driven by an eye solely on economic growth indicators such as GDP important to the rich has marginalised more than half a billion people who remain outside the formal economy. Despite the increasing economic growth and the size of the labour workforce, various estimates including the National Sample Survey report that India continues to employ around 80% to 90%[23] of its labour workforce in the informal sector since the liberalisation of the 1990s. In this period of rapid economic growth, the absolute number of people who joined the unorganised sector outnumbered those joining the organised sector, even in the high acceleration period between 2004-2012.[24] This means that while jobs have been created most of them have not been high paying or formal. The result is a large informal sector comprising a highly vulnerable labour force. The unprecedented growth in output in the economy has not led to a process of structural change in employment

THE JOB WORLD

How India compares with the world in providing decent employment to its people

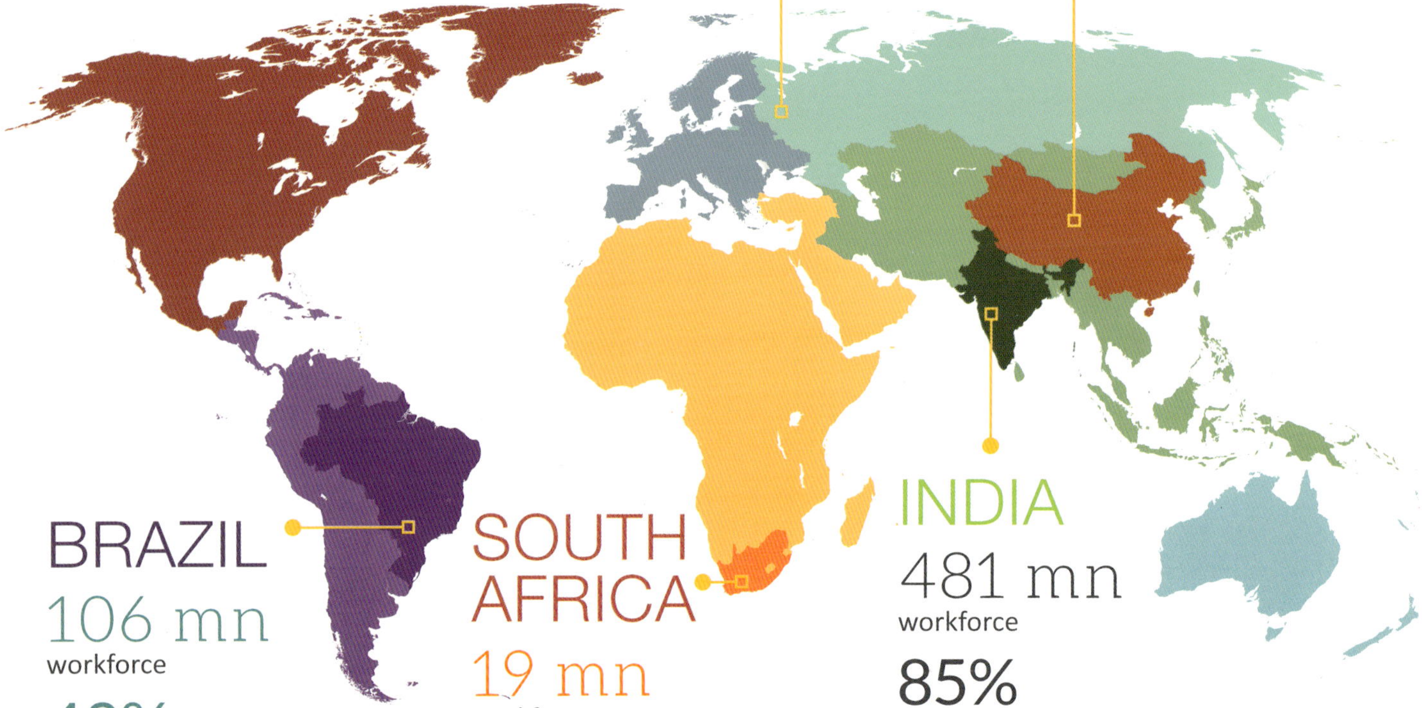

RUSSIA
76 mn
workforce
12%

CHINA
793 mn
workforce
32%

BRAZIL
106 mn
workforce
42%

SOUTH AFRICA
19 mn
workforce
32%

INDIA
481 mn
workforce
85%

Per cent employment in the informal economy (in non-agriculture employment)

Sources: Based on data from international labour Organisation, 2012
World Bank, 2011-14

The highest priority are placed on the needs of the formal sector such as attracting more foreign direct investment, raising stock market indices and manufacturing for exports. The actual needs of the workforce are reflected by the numbers working in the informal sector.

Adapted from The Indian Express, 2013

WORKFORCE & GDP CONTRIBUTION BY SECTOR

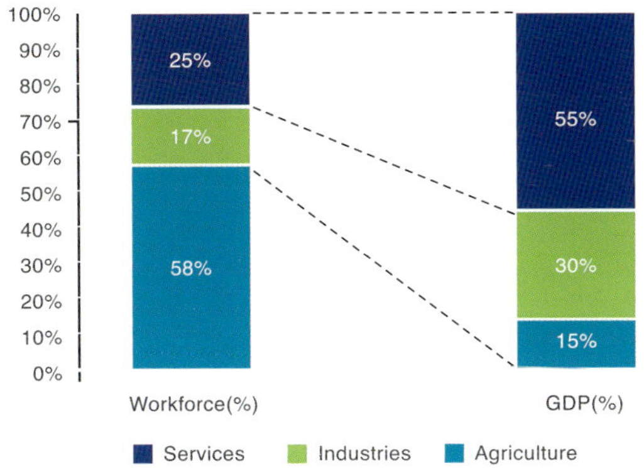

Source: Census of India, 2011

outside the agriculture sector for the Indian economy, as one would expect.[25] Among the major sectors of the economy, industry and services have grown much faster than agriculture, so the share of agriculture in GDP has naturally fallen rapidly. Furthermore, with factories becoming more and more mechanised, far faster than the farms, the difference in productivity between industry and agriculture is increasing over time. This increase of relative productivity in industry vis a vis agriculture, of course, led to substantial widening of the gap between industrial and agricultural wages.[26] The resulting wage differential promotes increased migration from rural to urban areas; a tendency somewhat reduced by the poor living conditions and inadequate job opportunities in urban spaces. The declining incentives for agriculture workers to stay on farm along with the declining productivity in the sector is also becoming a major threat to the nation's food and nutritional security.

The jobless nature of our economy's growth has set alarm bells ringing for those deeply concerned with securing a better future for the country. The reasons are manifold. What is evident is that the elegant trickle-down theory, of neoliberal economics, that the poor will automatically be better off as they benefit from the expanding opportunities created by the rich getting richer. As 65 years of independence and 25 years of economic "liberalisation" have shown, the crumbs that fall off the tables of the rich are really not enough to reverse the trends of growing inequality, atleast not in the Indian context. The gap between the rich and poor has only widened in the last decades. The expenditure share of the top 1 per cent of India's population increased from 6.5 per cent in 1993 to 9 per cent in 2010. India's top 5 per cent of the population spends 21.3 per cent of the total expenditure as against the 17.7 per cent in 1993.[27]

This form of development, which creates more and more people who are jobless and excluded from the mainstream

INEQUALITY IN INDIA: **BAD AS EVER**

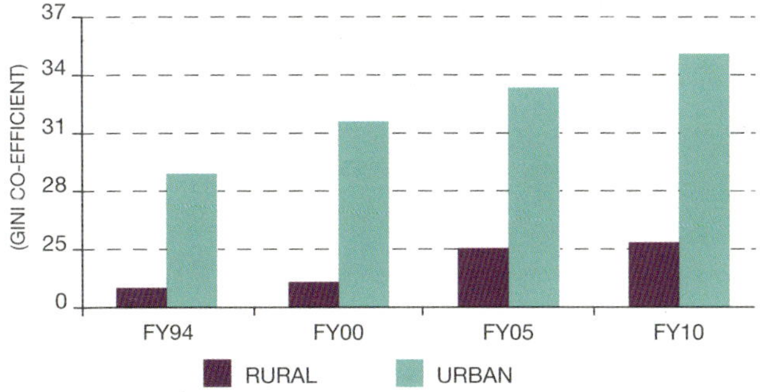

100% Perfect Inequality
0% Perfect Equality

Source: Livemint, 2011

MORE OR LESS EQUAL

Gini coefficient*

> "In India, the net worth of the billionaire community increased 12-fold in 15 years, enough to eliminate absolute poverty in the country twice over." Christine Lagarde

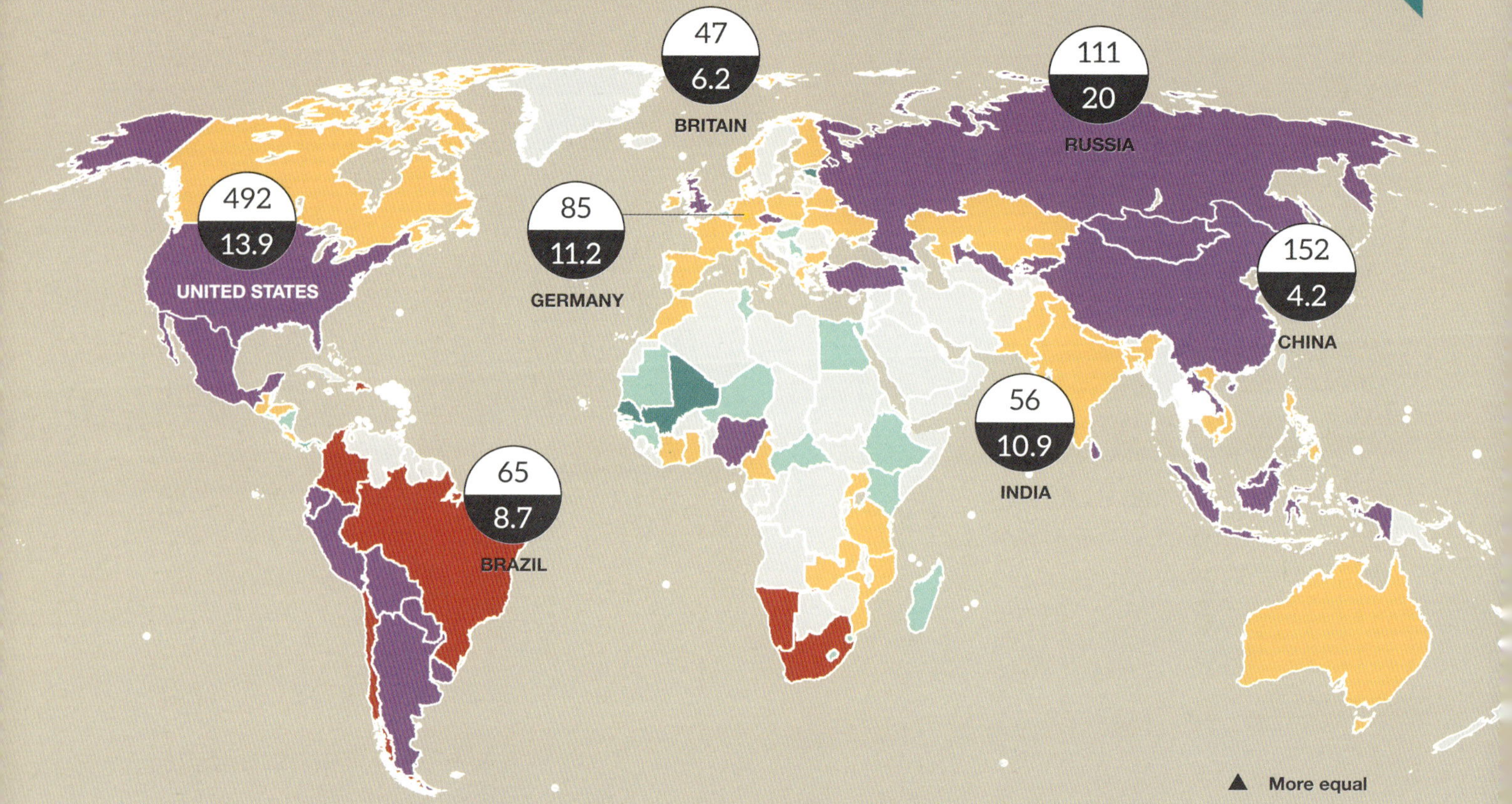

NUMBER OF BILLIONAIRES*

Net worth as % of GDP

▲ More equal

- 0 - 10%
- 10 - 20%
- 20 - 35%
- 35 - 50%
- > 50%

▼ More unequal

0=perfect equality

100=perfect inequality

Adapted from the Economist 2012 based on the Forbes Billionaires List, 2014

World Bank, Gini estimates (2010-2014)

HOW MUCH AND **WHAT ARE WE SUBSIDISING?**

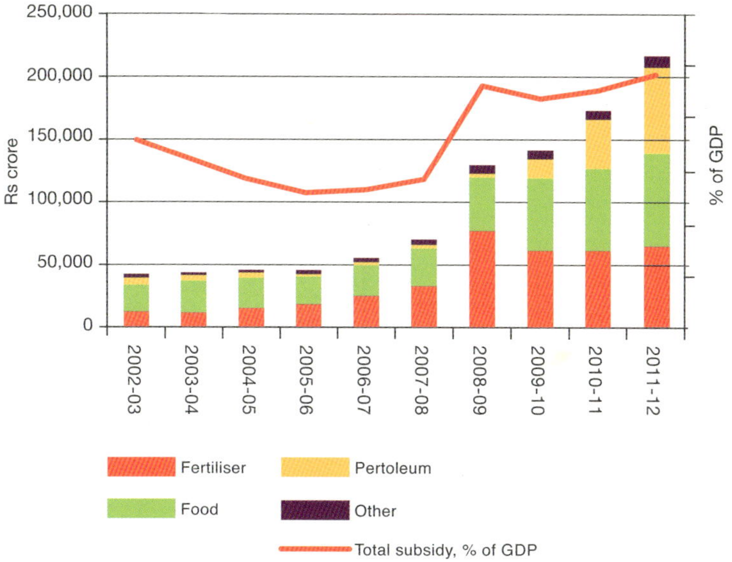

Source: PRS Legislative Research, 2012

economy, cannot be the basis of a sustainable democracy. On the contrary, it creates enormous dependencies among a large proportion of the population on the exchequers' doles and cash transfers. These subsidies, which have grown substantially in recent years, have severely squeezed the nation's budget and created a government that is so financially strapped that it can hardly make the investments in capacities and abilities of our people so essential for improving their future. This bias of the economy towards the rich few focuses largely on those investments that serve their interests. This bias largely ignores the need to create large numbers of jobs and regenerate the lost health of communities, limiting desirable economic and social transformation.

on the state of our ecosystem....

India's post 1947 development strategy has not only led to heightened poverty and income disparity, it has also degraded vast swaths of its natural capital, on which the majority of its people subsist. While India has made credible strides in promoting initiatives and systems for reduction in natural resource degradation and depletion, promotion of renewable materials, and climate change adaptation and mitigation, on almost every environmental parameter India's situation is already truly alarming.

While official statistics showcase an increase in forest cover, the reality may be different. There is now increasing concern regarding the assessment criteria as evidence suggests that the number is being over estimated as a bulk of the improvement results from correction in previous survey data and the changing definition of forest cover.[28] In fact, the details suggest India continues to lose quality forests - dense forests are degrading into scrub or sparsely covered forest areas in many states and open forests with low density of canopy have increased. Even with this, our forest cover falls short by 11.7 per cent of the widely acknowledged minimum requirement of 33 per cent of forest and tree cover for healthy ecology.[29] 25 per cent of India's total land is undergoing desertification while 32 per cent is facing degradation.[30]

Once the home of some of the world's mightiest rivers, India's water systems today are pale ghosts of their former glory. For the few that are still perennial, the pollution they carry has pretty much destroyed what they can contribute to the nation's cultural and economic life. Moreover, much of the shallow ground water of the country has been

INDIA'S ECOLOGICAL DEBT:
TIME TO REPAY?

BETWEEN 1990 AND 2010

GROUND WATER SUPPLIES IN INDIA'S BREADBASKET HAVE FALLEN 1 METER PER YEAR

Source: Columbia Water Centre, 2012

333
ACRES

An average of 135 hectares (333 acres) of forest land a day was given over for power, mining and other development projects in 2012-13

Source: Environment Impact and Assessment Resource and Response Centre, 2014

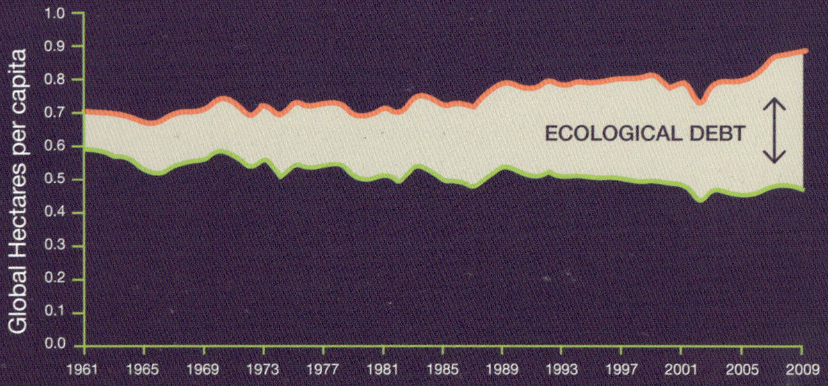

Source: Global Footprint Network 2010

CURRENT RESOURCE USE AT

70%

ABOVE OUR BIO CAPACITY

Ecological Footprint

Bio Capacity

INDIA'S MATERIAL DEMAND: WILL IT BE MET?

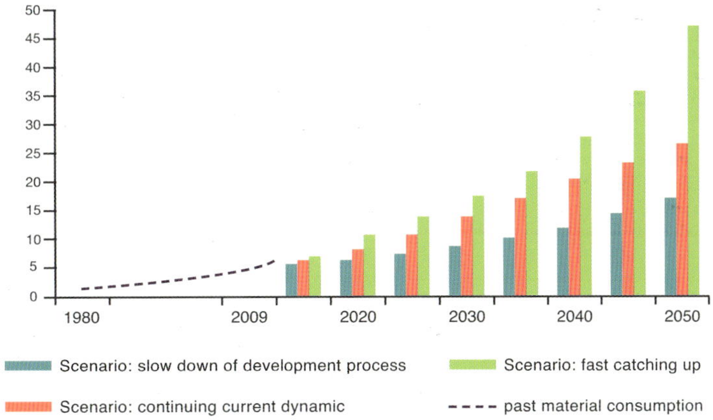

Source: Indo-German Environment Partnership, 2013

pumped, and satellite maps now show deeper, fossil and non-rechargeable aquifers under massive onslaught drawing down waters that had collected over millennia. With 70 per cent of surface water polluted and 60 per cent of groundwater sources expected to be in a critical state within the next decade, the impending water crisis is one of the major health, environmental and economic issue the country is likely to face in the short, medium and the long run.[31]

The loss of tree cover, the creation of land use systems prone to ever increasing floods and droughts, and resource extraction for materials has led to massive erosion of our highly fertile soils, increasing the threats to our food producing capacity. Adding to this, the combination of poorly designed irrigation systems and excessive use of chemicals is leading to huge losses of our rich arable lands which is having serious impacts on food security.

India stands at overshoot of 1.7 times its 0.5 gha/cap biocapacity. With a 0.9 gha/cap ecological footprint, we are now using our resources at a rate that is 70% above our bio-capacity.[32] If India continues its current development trajectory its "resource demand in 2030 will have more than tripled to a figure equivalent to the combined current consumption of all the OECD countries".[33]

These trends of degradation remained largely unnoticed until recently because of clever innovations that raised productivity and permitted substitutions but, as the limits to such measures are beginning to be reached, they are now showing up in uncontrolled price fluctuations for commodities, raw materials, and fuel. This is increasingly making their availability uncertain and raising the risks faced by governments and businesses in managing their operations. While the prices of most commodities were gradually declining for decades and centuries, since 2000 this trend has sharply reversed and now most commodity

India also finds itself in the midst of a dramatic journey of urbanisation.

800 million

people will eventually live in cities and yet as many will continue to live in rural areas by 2050, creating further stresses on our already fragile ecosystem.[19]

By 2030

1 million

The number of cities with over 1 million inhabitants will rise from 42 to 68

$1.2 trillion

Capital investment needed to finance infrastructure for India's cities

700-900 million

Square meters of commercial and residential space needs to be built annually - or a new Mumbai every year

2.5 billion

square metres of roads will have to be paved. 20 times the capacity added in the past decades

Source - McKinsey Global Institute, 2010

"Like a snake eating its own tail, our growth-orientated civilisation suffers from the delusion that there are no environmental limits to growth" - Samuel Alexander

GLOBAL PRICE RISE: PAYING THE COST

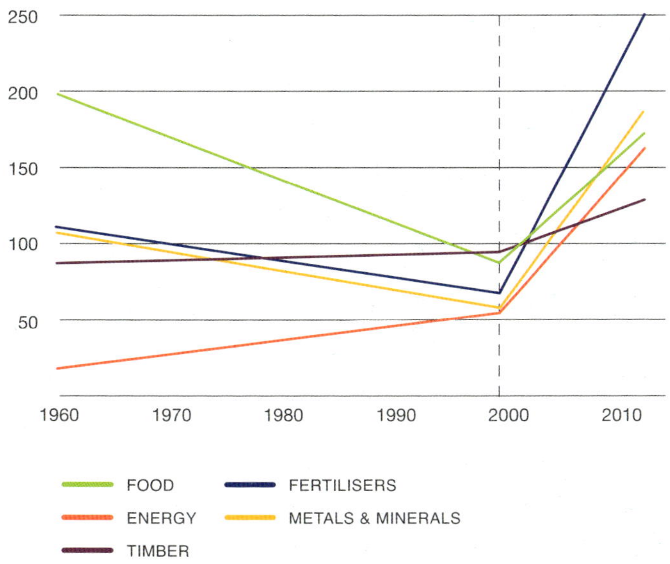

Source: World Resource Institute (using World Bank data), 2012

prices are rising every year in India and across the world, despite occasional, temporary re-reverses.

India also finds itself in the midst of a dramatic journey of urbanisation. By 2050, some 700 to 800 million[34] people will live in cities - 50% of the nation's population. The other side of the coin is that as many will also continue to live in rural areas by 2050, creating further stresses on our already fragile ecosystems, which are, of course, mostly in rural areas.

On the market demand side, the new era of consumerism, led mainly by India's elite and rising middle class, of profligate material consumption and the resulting generation of waste is underway. Propelled by the idea that more is better, there is now a growing and a near insatiable demand from those with the requisite purchasing power for an ever-expanding range of goods and services. On the supply side, the market tries to meet this demand by producing more and more "things", mindless of the impacts of this on the resource base or on the capacity of nature to absorb the resulting waste.

With growing urbanisation and paving over of highly fertile lands, increasing consumerism, and setting aside lands for mines, dams, factories, the side effects of the development choices we have made are massive degradation of our environmental resources, with very worrying implications for the future of our economy and the lives of the generations that follow us.

Do We Need a New Development Model?

If these trends continue for much longer, and inequality keeps growing, a large part of the population, which cannot afford the prevailing prices, will soon lose the ability to buy what is produced. While productivity of the industrial and agricultural sectors will continue to rise, the incomes of the vast majority won't – a phenomenon that is now increasingly apparent in the economies of the West – not just countries such as Greece and Spain but even Japan and USA. As such a stage approaches, economies hit or transgress various societal boundaries, which often lead to large scale disruptions, taking the economy point where it many collapse taking down with it the demand for products and services as they are no longer affordable.

Moreover, since the natural resource base, without which the human economy would not exist, is at best finite and in terms of what can be cost-effectively extracted from it, very limited. Creating more supply means mining more resources, which in turn means generating more disruptions in our life support systems. Mother Nature is, up to a limit, hugely bounteous and resilient but being a vast, finely tuned system, with highly complex linkages and feedback systems, beyond a threshold - that with our present knowledge is often difficult to foresee - she can also become quite vulnerable and break down rather suddenly. The science of climate change is just beginning to show how suddenly and how much. This is just is the beginning because the other missing link, relating to the limits of the societal operating space and its interactions with environmental ones could be enough to lead to total breakdown in the life support systems.

As time goes on, a highly inequitable and consumerism-based society tends to run into the wall of unsustainability. Economic forces will automatically kick in to limit demand and ecological forces will automatically force limits on supply. The new market equilibrium can then only be at a much lower level than anyone, even the most ardent conservationist, can wish for. The post Keynesian reaction to such a situation is to revive the economy by stimulating consumption, in the hope that it will generate a virtuous, upward cycle of more demand... creating more supply... creating more purchasing power... creating more demand... ad infinitum... till the next, even bigger bust.

Developing technology for a country like India in order to go on consuming the way industrialised countries have been for the last century is a dead-end and we can only expect to face another meltdown (like the 2008 financial crisis) only more speedily and severely. While these challenges are occasionally recognised by some policy makers, the short-term considerations that dominate the thinking ensure that both elected governments and result oriented corporate managers have strong professional incentives to ignore them.

It is not our contention that no development should take place. However, we uphold that an alternative form of development, where the benefits of our freedom benefit and reach all, must be adopted with great vigour for improving the lives of the growing population. India is at a critical juncture. While a few of our fellow citizens have benefitted greatly from the growth of our economy, the current trajectory of development is showing unmistakeable signs of shaking the foundations of wellbeing and prosperity of our natural and human capital. There is both a feeling of despair and of hope about our future and how we think about our past. India is perhaps at that interesting juncture where we NEED NOT make the mistakes of the others.

Ideally, we should be able to short-circuit the process by which most countries in the past went from being unequal, poor and dirty, through intermediate steps of being hugely unequal, very rich and extremely dirty, to a final situation after many decades of becoming generally equitable, rich and clean. India needs to tunnel through this inverted U-shaped curve by designing a development strategy that combines community, environmental and economic goals to achieve a sustainable national future. It must empower its communities and civil society with information and

TUNNELING THROUGH TO NEW OPPORTUNITIES

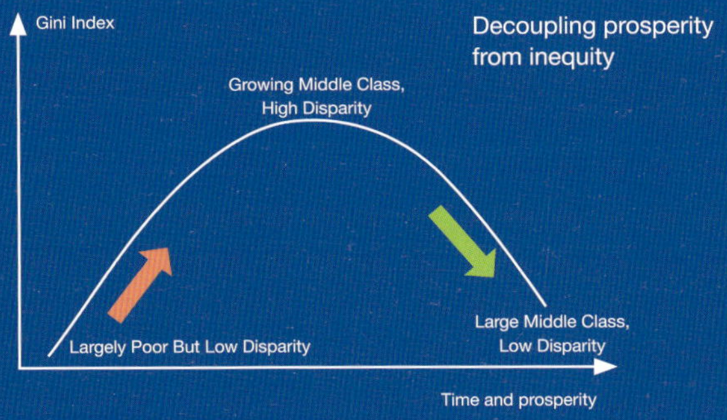

THE CLASSICAL KUZNETS CURVE OF INCOME DISTRIBUTION

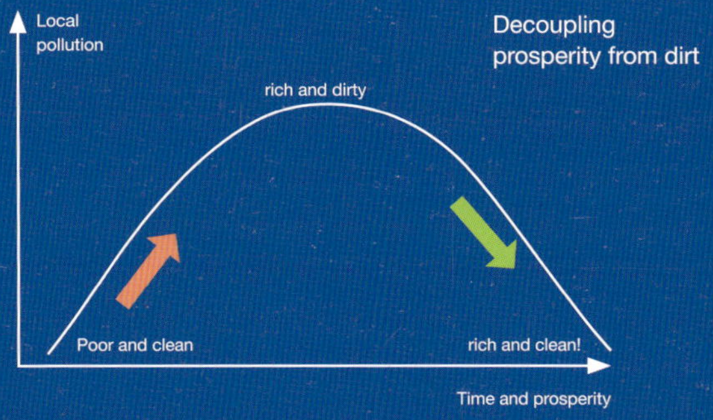

TRANSLATING THE DECOUPLING IDEA TO ENVIRONMENT
THE KUZNETS-CURVE OF LOCAL POLLUTION

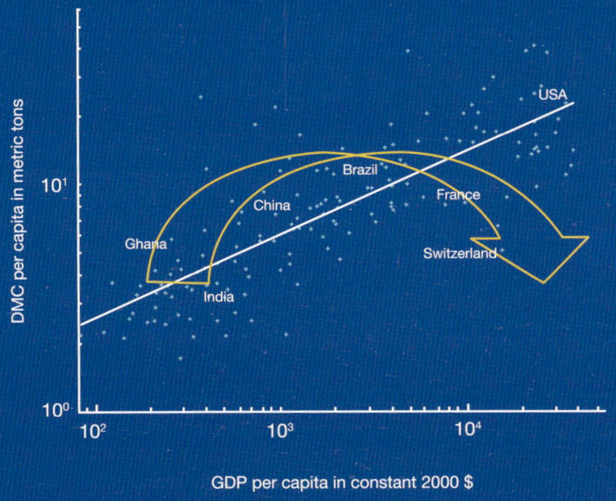

CREATING THE KUZNETS CURVE FOR RESOURCE USE MEANS INTENTIONAL INCREASE OF RESOURCE PRODUCTIVITY

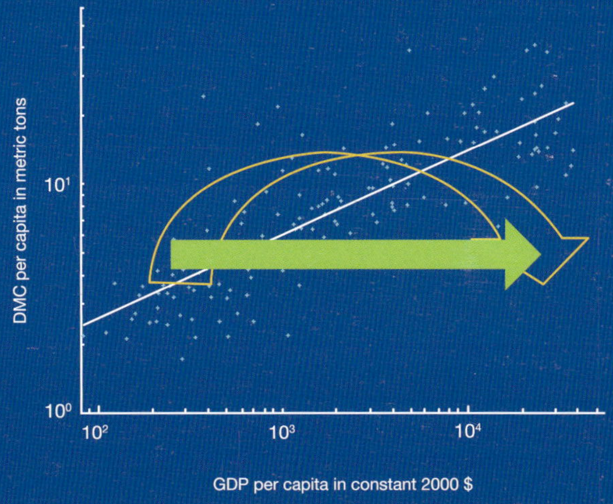

... AND ASSISTING DEVELOPING COUNTRIES TO TUNNEL THROUGH

Source: Ernst Von Weizsaecker, 2012

enable them to voice the interests of the poor and the nature in the world driven by the vested interests of a few. India cannot stay afloat for long, if the leaks at one end of the ship of state keep on growing. The answers provided by political leaders, practitioners, and professional researchers have been highly complicated and arcane. The real answers are, in fact, quite simple, though they might need fairly complex and strategic interventions. At a time when India's natural resource base is poised between collapse and sustainability, the country has to seize the opportunity to show a new path towards sustainable development.

> "Choices have to be made - some will be easy, others quite hard"

INDIA

PULLING TOGETHER OR **PUSHING APART?**

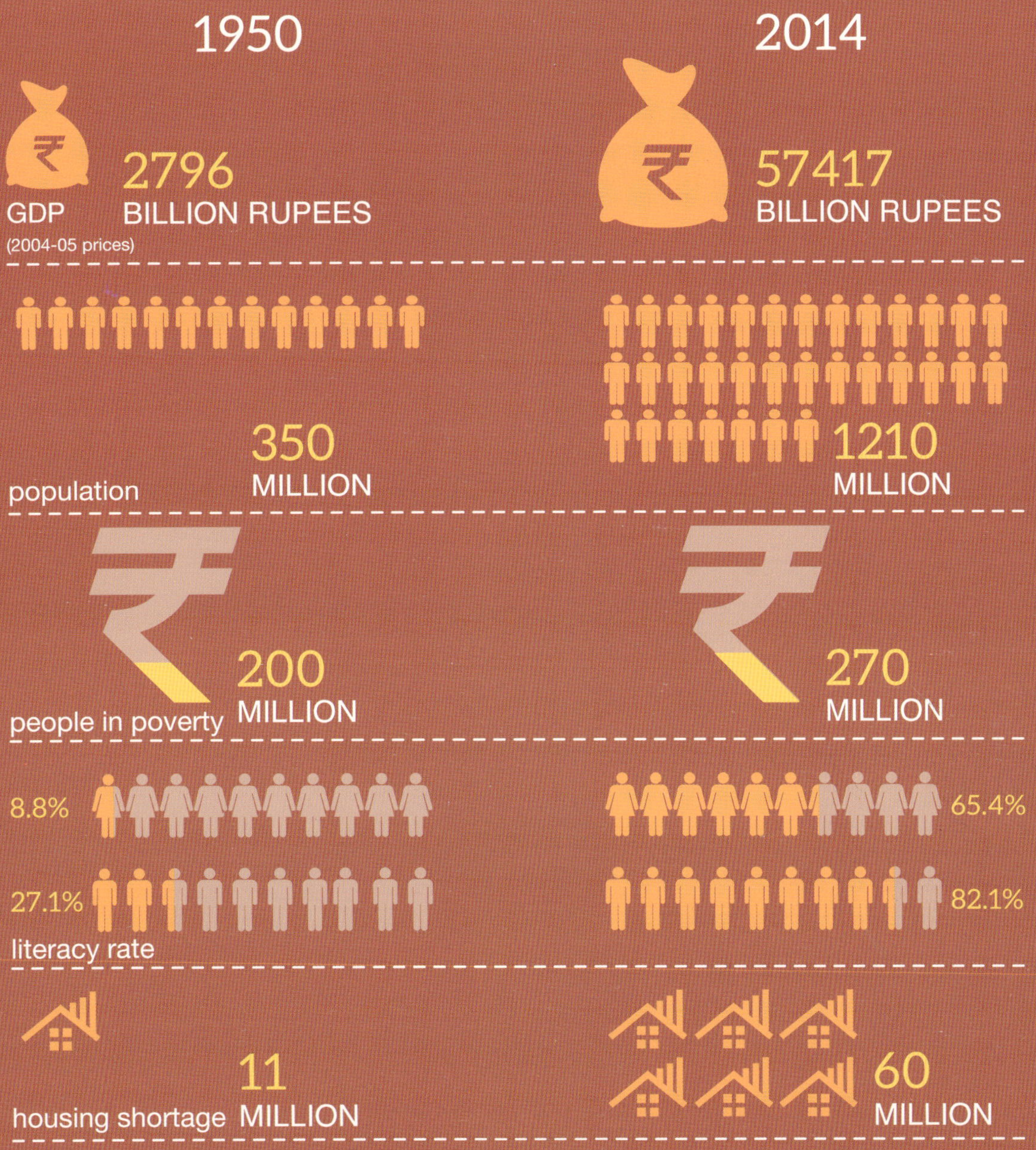

Sources: Planning Commission, Census of India, Central Statistical Organisation

03

ALTERNATIVE
Pathways

The future is ours to choose

The future we get depends on which of the four alternative pathways we decide to take

COPY CAT

PIGGY BACK

LEAP FROG

HORSE JUMP

ALTERNATIVE PATHWAYS

The Future is Ours to Choose

Evolving Pathways for India

Forecasting the future is an ancient practice common to most civilisations. Today's futurologists rely on more modern and sophisticated methods to explore the trends and directions of the economy, society and issues of human concern. These methods range from building broad-brush scenarios based on reasonable assumptions to detailed analysis of sophisticated systems models using carefully validated sectoral data.

Mathematical models, such as those used in the rigorous science of system dynamics, using detailed biophysical and socio-economic data can provide powerful insights into the future outcomes of present decisions. However, their very precision often acts against their reliability as predictors because of the uncertainties and unknowns that exist in the real world, which can quite easily emerge unexpectedly and derail their conclusions. Moreover, they can be complicated, requiring sophisticated training to create and interpret, so they are often not fully accessible to either decision makers or the lay public. There is, therefore, also great value in studying less precisely defined, holistic 'scenarios' for a wider understanding of the broad contours of how the future will or could unfold.

Two better-known and trend-setting scenario exercises come from the Global Scenario Group (GSG) and the Shell Oil Company, who have been working for several decades on analysing world futures based on different assumptions. The most recent Shell Scenario is based on two 'lenses', Mountains and Oceans, with two different regulatory regimes involving different relative balance between the involvement of government and the private sector in decision-making. Shell Scenario exercises in the past have been more catholic in their choice of assumptions and treatment of wider socio-economic policy concerns and have delivered deep insights into the way current decisions impact a broad spectrum of future outcomes.

The GSG exercises have over the years, homed in on three broad groups of scenarios, each with two alternative sets of assumptions. These are, more or less in self-explanatory descriptions:

Conventional Worlds (Business as usual, Markets, New technologies, No major surprises)

- **Market Forces:** Reliance on the invisible hand of the market
- **Policy Reform:** Continually promoting sustainability

Barbarisation (If no corrective action is taken on present trends)

- **Breakdown:** The world descends into conflict and collapse
- **Fortress World:** Environment collapses, elites retreat to enclaves, others exist in poverty

The Great Transition (Changes in societal values, Materialism/greed decline, Solidarity rises)

- **Eco-Communalism:** Localism, environmental ethic, strong civil society
- **New Sustainability Paradigm:** Lower population, consumerism, and environmental footprint

These and other scenario building exercises are of great value in helping evaluate the consequences of the way the future is currently unfolding and in designing a different one, should such change be considered desirable.

The problem with the scenario method is, of course, that the reliability and therefore value of scenarios lies in how well they are tailored to the context of the issues in hand. A global scenario for the economics of metals, for example, can be a straightforward and very accurate analysis because the objective of the exercise and the data needed can be precisely defined. A national scenario for sustainable development, particularly for a mixed economy such as that of India is a highly complex task. It involves making assumptions and judgments that can assess the implications of wealth and incomes ranging from tremendous affluence to extreme poverty; ecosystems from warm tropical islands to freezing Himalayan mountains; and cultures ranging from indigenous communities in remote forests to cosmopolitans in the biggest of cities.

One thing is clear, that identifying the kind of future a society considers desirable and how such a future is to be achieved requires knowledge of the aspirations of all members of that society. In particular, for a viable, sustainable democracy, priority attention must be given to the needs of those who live at the margins of society. Western activism addressing the circumstances of over-affluent populations which over-extract rapidly depleting resources from nature may well be justified in calling for a 'simpler life', doing with less and cutting back on waste. However, for the very poor – of whom there are several hundred million in India, with few of them voluntarily producing much waste – such responses can begin to make sense only after the basic needs of every citizen have been met.

Drawing lessons from 30 years of work on sustainable national development, and other scenario work of the type just described, DA presents here some basic scenarios of the future to enable the people and decision makers of our country consciously to choose among possible pathways that will lead to sustainable outcomes in the least possible time – for the greatest common benefit at least overall cost. The primary goal of our effort has been to identify a pathway that will lead, sooner than later, to India becoming a sustainable economy and society – in which no one is left behind and where our environmental resource base becomes and continues to be healthy and productive. The purpose of DA's work on understanding the alternative forms India's future may take is not an end in itself but rather a first step towards designing the tools and the means by which the nation can plan its future to be vibrant and sustainable. The scenarios we present here have been developed to enable us to state our assumptions clearly, assess the implications and challenge our thinking on India's current development trajectory and consider its implications for us and for coming generations.

To make the analysis of our future clearer and more accessible, we use four simple metaphors and storylines to develop a set of possible alternative pathways for India in its run up from the present to its first centenary as a nation:

1. Can India continue as a ***Copycat*** nation, with its current ***business as usual (BAU)*** approach — single-mindedly, unquestioningly chasing economic growth in a social environment characterised by rampant inequality, runaway consumerism and ruinous devastation of nature? Such a base scenario can lead only, inexorably and rather quickly, to outcomes that are unsustainable and, in short order, unstable or self-destructive. At some point, surely within the working life of today's youth, people and nature will be forced to fight back, leading to social, environmental and demographic pressures that will automatically trigger an economic reversal – the typical outcome for unbalanced or lopsided systems of ***overshoot and collapse***.

2. Or will India be able to ***Piggyback*** - to extract useful lessons from across the world, to introduce ***incremental change*** or ***fine-tune*** present practices and reorient them towards greater sustainability? Can we broaden our thinking enough to select and emulate best practices, adapted to the needs of our own resource endowments and cultural aspirations? Will we initiate policy reforms that comprehensively combine the innovation and efficiencies of the marketplace and the scaling-out potential of the private sector with the social objectives and environment responsibilities of the public sector and civil society? This is a minimum requirement for any socio-economic system that can both ***eliminate poverty*** and ***regenerate the natural resource base***, although it cannot guarantee truly permanent sustainability.

3. Given the urgency of the social, economic and environmental threats facing the nation, can India reach the most desirable stage – ***Leapfrog***? In the view of a growing body of opinion, including that of Development Alternatives, India now has to introduce a ***basic shift*** in its societal goals, policies, institutions and technology choices to enable it to make the deep transitions needed for achieving ***sustainable economic and social success***. What will it take for India to design effective new solutions that are right for its people and for its natural endowment even if they involve temporary/transitional handicaps in a world that is globalised and highly competitive?

4. Ultimately, in the face of rapidly growing populations and economic activities on the one hand and diminishing social resilience and natural resource availability on the other, we will have to make some fundamental shifts in our development choices to prevent human civilisation from being prematurely terminated. These shifts, needing really transformative societal change, nothing less than a ***Horsejump***, will necessarily involve ***structural transformation*** in all spheres -- technology choices, lifestyles, institutions of governance and societal values – which can enable us to fulfil our destiny as the primary species on our planet, taking responsibility for all other living things. Such a jump could give new meaning to the Anthropocene, a new geological era when humanity goes beyond the dominance of the environment to ***living in harmony*** with nature.

The value of this 'Development Alternatives' Menagerie' is that it is easy to understand and remember – and to argue over, enabling the dialogue to be based on clearly defined assumptions. It can help conceptualise, clarify and communicate persuasively to people of all ages, callings and levels – school children, teachers, academics, civil society professionals, development practitioners, media persons, faith leaders, business persons, government officials, and political decision makers. While we recognise that this terminology flows easily in English, and that it may not be easy to translate into other languages, we feel that the value for understanding, recall and communication of these metaphors makes them worth sharing here.

Each scenario describes the nature and degree of change required from existing practice, but its characteristics cannot be described precisely for all circumstances, so it is important to note that there is some overlap of attributes as one scenario merges and yields to the next higher one.

COPY CAT SCENARIO

Business as Usual

In this pathway, India will continue to tread its current development practices and trajectory, emulating development patterns followed earlier by economies of the global North.

Driven by the simple domination of a neoliberal economic philosophy, faith of decision makers will continue to reside in market prices to take care of scarcities, continuous substitution of resources, and improved productivity through innovation. In this scenario, environmental and societal wellbeing will play second fiddle to the goals of the market.

The continuous chasing, indeed maximising, GDP growth and financial numbers on *Dalal* Street will perpetuate centralisation of industry, domination of the big business agenda and jobless growth – economic systems benefiting only the rich. While an impetus is provided to the wider economy through large-scale capital expenditures, the myopic view of what the nation needs most will deepen the schisms, rendering the already fragile system unsustainable. The underlying mindset will be "More is Better" and the time horizon for decisions is short at best. Continuing on this pathway will create a cycle of exploding acquisition and resource exploitation by a few and rampant growth of unfulfilled basic needs and impoverishment for most.

While profit maximising and cost cutting imperatives of the marketplace are likely to lead to some productivity improvements, the main engines of the economy (in addition to agriculture) would continue to be industries based on physical and mechanical processes and would generate some incremental rise in rated efficiency. Consumerism (acquiring more things), the brown (using polluting and dirty technologies), and the linear (descending one way from cradle to grave) will dominate industrial thinking. With planetary boundaries being increasingly transgressed, the business as usual scenario is likely to result in further loss of livelihoods, increasing vulnerabilities, price volatility, and unprecedented material use. Resources will be locked into coping with disruption and destruction leading to an environmental breakdown. This, along with stunted structural development will create social strife and conflict – paving the way for serious trouble.

India will desperately seek reforms but will be locked into a policy paralysis. Development interventions will give too much focus on outputs without addressing the roots causes and nurturing transformations. For instance, there will be less emphasis on creating jobs for poverty alleviation and more on doles and transfers. On one hand there will be creation of dependencies with no incentives for entrepreneurship and innovation, on the other it will create a cash-strapped government leading to a fiscal drain and increased economic vulnerabilities like inflation, income inequality, and raised deficits further slowing growth. Piecemeal reforms will overlook coordinated and systemic solutions for real reforms – creating dichotomies and tensions.

The simple advantages that make Copycat - BAU an attractive tactical approach is that it is easy, within the comfort zone of most major actors, requires no difficult decision or financial investment and is simple to sell to the public. Since the costs of inaction are generally deferred to a point in the future that is beyond the forthcoming quarterly statement or the next election, neither business nor government is likely to promote a change. This is usually the default outcome.

If continued along this pathway, in a few decades, we can expect to witness a severe overshoot and collapse - bringing progress to a halt. All in all, India will continue to reduce overall resilience leading us into a complex web of multiple crises and defunct economic, social, and ecological systems.

PIGGY BACK

Fine Tuning

In thinking through how to transition from the present, dead-end Copycat path we are on, the first step is to make incremental changes based on best practices and tested models developed domestically or elsewhere. Piggyback is an important stage in any systematic effort to reorient a national economy towards sustainability.

In terms of values and systems, the conventional desire to economic growth will still prevail. Faith will continue to reside in market forces and policy makers will be open to synergies that can come from acting in complementarity with other ministries or businesses to align with the goals of sustainable development.

In a large domestic economy such as that of India, it will involve supporting domestic innovation capacity (in academic, private and public sector institutions) and having the ability to identify, negotiate, adapt and adopt best practices from across the world aimed at raising resource productivity and lowering pollution and environmental damage. For example, India could potentially adopt practices like renewable energy from Germany, water management from Israel, forest management from Korea, biodiversity conservation from Canada. Such a fine tuning approach, involving acquisition of the best models and technologies from across the globe is desirable and will certainly encourage reorientation of the economy towards a more sustainable direction but is unlikely to create fundamental transformation in the polity or economy.

Piggyback strategies would phase the transition from brown to green industrial technologies; they would entail a switch in production systems over to more chemistry-based industrial methods creating an incremental jump to the domain of potential efficiency, i.e., ***what would be possible***, if small changes involving minor capital investment were to be made – such as normal debottlenecking measures, and industrial engineering, among others. The philosophy of some of our decision makers and their advisors will rest on the assumption that rapid economic growth is the primary requirement to reduce the ranks of the poor, improve social and economic equity and reduce conflict. Decision makers at the other end of the political spectrum will assume that more important than growth is the need for mechanisms to distribute the existing economic pie more evenly throughout the population. At the stage of Piggyback, both markets and public sector will be essential for enabling technological innovation and policy support will be available to enable incremental change to flow smoothly.

In this scenario, a society can achieve reductions in resource consumption and environmental impact of up to factors of five (5X). This is doable today, with adaptations of existing processes through technology and strategy. The basic mindset of this phase of the transition to sustainability is “More from Less” and the time horizon of decisions is at most in years. However, while such transformations are necessary, Piggyback interventions are not likely to be enough to reach truly sustainable futures.

LEAP FROG

Deep Changes for a New Economy

If neither today's BAU methods, nor incremental changes in them through fine-tuning are enough to take us to true sustainability, clearly there follows a need for some kind of a quantum leap that will bring about the level of change required. The third tier of change, Leapfrog, is intended to achieve just that, while leading to outcomes that are humanistic and ecologically sensitive.

Moving beyond the limits of Piggyback pathways, Leapfrog interventions include raising the floors (fulfilling basic human needs), which on a finite resource base cannot be realised without lowering the ceilings (consuming towards sufficiency) and plugging the leaks (conserving resources, minimising waste).

A defining feature of the Leapfrog era will be the growing recognition of the close and continuing interdependence of human and ecological systems. Overthrowing the conventional devotion to economic growth, development will be measured by what genuinely contributes to societal goals, which are carefully specified by participative processes. By treating the economy as a sub-set of the ecosystem, and financial capital as subservient to real natural, social, human, and physical capital, this pathway will lead to a deep change – transforming objectives and principles for the wellbeing of the people and planet.

Reflected in both concept and practice by the widespread agreement, economics and engineering will be treated as a means for achieving wellbeing of people and planet, and not ends in themselves.

Leapfrog strategies will embrace green solutions for the economy. Adding to the physical and chemical focus of production systems inherited from earlier phases, new technologies based on biological processes, maximising reuse and recycling and minimising waste,will be mainstreamed. This will need a quantum jump to the domain of latent efficiency, i.e., what should be possible, if significant changes involving substantial capital investment and behaviour change were to be made – such as product life extension, miniaturisation and sharing of underutilised assets. By Leapfrogging, a society can achieve reductions in resource consumption and environmental impact of up to a factor of ten (10X) or more. The basic mindset of this phase of the transition to sustainability is "Much

More from Much Less" and the time horizon of decisions is at least in decades or a human lifetime. Companies will no longer view value creation through the narrow lens of financial performance over short time scales, but look to create long-term shared value for both business and society. These new mindsets will foster a highly diversified economy rooted in strong local economies and green livelihoods that advance the goals of sustainability and human fulfillment. For a few industries such as oil refineries, steel mills and and sea ports, economies of scale and technological imperatives may dictate the setting up of large, centralised units, many others, including power generation and food processing may be more amenable to smaller decentralised scales. Industry will therefore include diverse portfolios of mini, small, medium and large enterprises located across regions guided by the commitment to create profits for their investors and long-term shared value for all stakeholders. Social enterprises are important in the future of this sustainable economy. That such a shift is achievable is clearly evidenced by recent experience that taking a long-term and holistic perspective on value creation and a collaborative approach outperforms the hunt for purely short-term benefits. Both public and private sectors will have to increasingly view and measure growth and value differently.

During the era of Leapfrog, our societies will be more inclusive, equitable and prosperous than they are in the hierarchical traditional systems and class systems of today. Ecological and sustainable resource management will build the resilience of those depending on natural resources for their livelihoods.

Systemic, collaborative, and integrated approaches will help break the silos and facilitate strong fundamental connections possible in local, participative decisions systems and micro-level policies and programmes. Forward thinking and informed policy-making will weigh the costs of indirect and long-term environmental impacts. Governance in this scenario will be conducted through a web of government, civil society, and business nodes at national, state and local levels, always acting in partnership with democracy, participation and accountability at its heart. This will entail a more effective and responsive attitude towards the needs of the communities otherwise marginalised by the traditional top-down approach.

HORSE JUMP

Structural Transformation

While the deep changes introduced in the Leapfrog economy will hopefully be adequate to reset societal processes and restart them on the road to a sustainable future, the precautionary principle dictates that we still have to allow for any risks that might be thrown up by unforeseen exigencies, unexpected obstacles, unlikely but potentially huge black swan events and the generally hostile universe of unknown unknowns.

Given that not one of the big planetary issues which today engage the undivided attention of the world's heads of state at various summits every couple of years (climate change, biodiversity loss, environmental destruction) was considered a threat 25 years ago, it is difficult to imagine that no new sudden threats will appear in the next 25 years, much less by the end of the century.

To create a genuinely sustainable future, the fourth tier of change, Horsejump, is intended to put the global economy in a truly safe operating space. In doing so it will enable humanity to achieve its full and genuine potential while leaving for future generations, the possibility of the widest conceivable options for choosing their own paths to fulfilment. The Horsejump era is one of wholly new set of societal values and aspirations that lead to structural transformations of perceptions and potentials. Societies will live by a fundamentally different economics, ethics and relationship with their environment. The defining feature of this era will be a firm commitment from all in society to embed human civilisation as an integral part of the biosphere, with a fuller understanding of the mutual interdependence between the people and ecosystems. Today's institutions of governance, business, and civil society will dissolve into hybrids with multi-purpose, multi-attribute functions.

For the economy, Horsejump strategies will embrace blue solutions[35], relying increasingly on biomimicry whereby nature itself or technologies inspired by nature become the dominant basis for producing industrial goods and services and agricultural crops. Such a circular economy takes reuse and recycling to higher levels of refurbishing and remanufacturing, both to minimise extraction of virgin resources and production of waste. This would need a discontinuous jump to the domain of systemic efficiency, i.e., what could be possible, if significant changes involving natural technologies, consumer and producer behaviour were to be made, though the capital investment required may not be much. Product life extension, miniaturisation and sharing of underutilised assets will be supplemented by a 'performance economy' approach in which products are paid for by the service they provide rather than being owned. Although there are not many examples yet that can provide empirical evidence, a Horsejump should be able to achieve very substantial reductions in resource consumption and environmental impact – perhaps as much as a factor of twenty (20X) or more. The basic mindset of this phase of the transition to sustainability is "A Great Deal from Very Little and Less from Less where necessary" and the time horizon of decisions is at least inter-generational.

Horsejump societies will be be able to further improve on the environmental, social and economic advantages of those in the Leapfrog phase.

PATHWAYS FOR INDIA

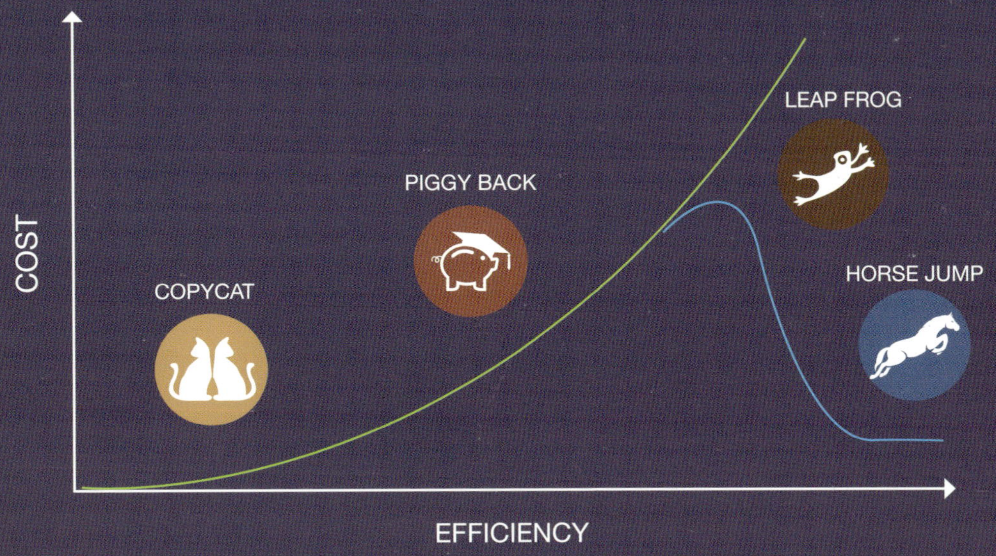

We would like to emphasise that the goal of this scenario building is to provide an insight into the future. It is not intended as a prediction of the future of India but to support informed policy and rational action for designing and building a sustainable one. These scenarios show that if the Indian economy is to flourish and the benefits it brings are to go to everyone in the country, we will have to very substantially change the way we choose our technologies, design our institutions, particularly our financial systems, and the way we relate to nature. A sustainable world will need a more socially just, environmentally sound and economically efficient form of development than the one being widely pursued today. In order to understand the scenarios better we demonstrate the use among the different potential communities of users.

MENAGERIE OF CHOICES

Pathways	*Ideology*	*Dominant Actors*	*Level of Efficiency Dematerialisation*	*Technology Basis*	*Societal Choices*	*Instruments*	*Outcomes*	*Time Horizons*
Business as Usual	More is better	Markets	Rated Efficiency	Physics & Mechanics	Technology	Fiscal Taxes, Incentives	What Is	Short
Copycat			1X					Unsustainable
Piggyback	More from Less	Markets	Potential	Chemistry	Strategies	Case Studies	What Would Be	Medium
Fine Tuning		Government & Policy	5X			Best Practices		Temporary (little investment)
Leapfrog	Much more from Much Less	Government & Policy	Latency	Biology	Objectives and Principles	Statutory	What Should Be	Lifetime
Behaviour, Innovation & Deep Change		CSOs	10X			Regulatory		Sustainable (more investment)
Horse jump	A great deal from Less/ Less from Less	Citizen Community	Systemic Capacity	Social Lifestyle	Values	Behaviour	What Could Be	Intergenerational
Aspirations & Structural Change			20X			Education/ wisdom		Regenerative (major investment)

Pathways	Business			Domestic			
	Manufacturing	Construction	Waste	Lighting	Cooking	Water	Transport
Copycat	Hardware	Cement, Steel, Concrete	Dumping, Incineration	Incandescent, Fluorescent	Electric Plate	Leak Control	Car, Airplanes
Piggyback	Miniaturisation, Longevity	Lightweight Elements	Composting, Recycling	CFLs	Gas, Pressure Cooker	Low Flow, Front-Loading Wash M/c	Fuel efficient cars, Hybrid
Leapfrog	Remanufacturing & Service Economy	Recycled Materials	Biogas, Reuse	LEDs	Microwave	Recycle	Public Transport, Bicycles Airships
Horsejump	Bio-mimicry	Industrial Wastes	Refuse	Daylight	Enzymatic	Self-Cleaning Polymers/ Skins	Walking, Zoning, localisation

VISUALISING **THE FOUR SCENARIOS**

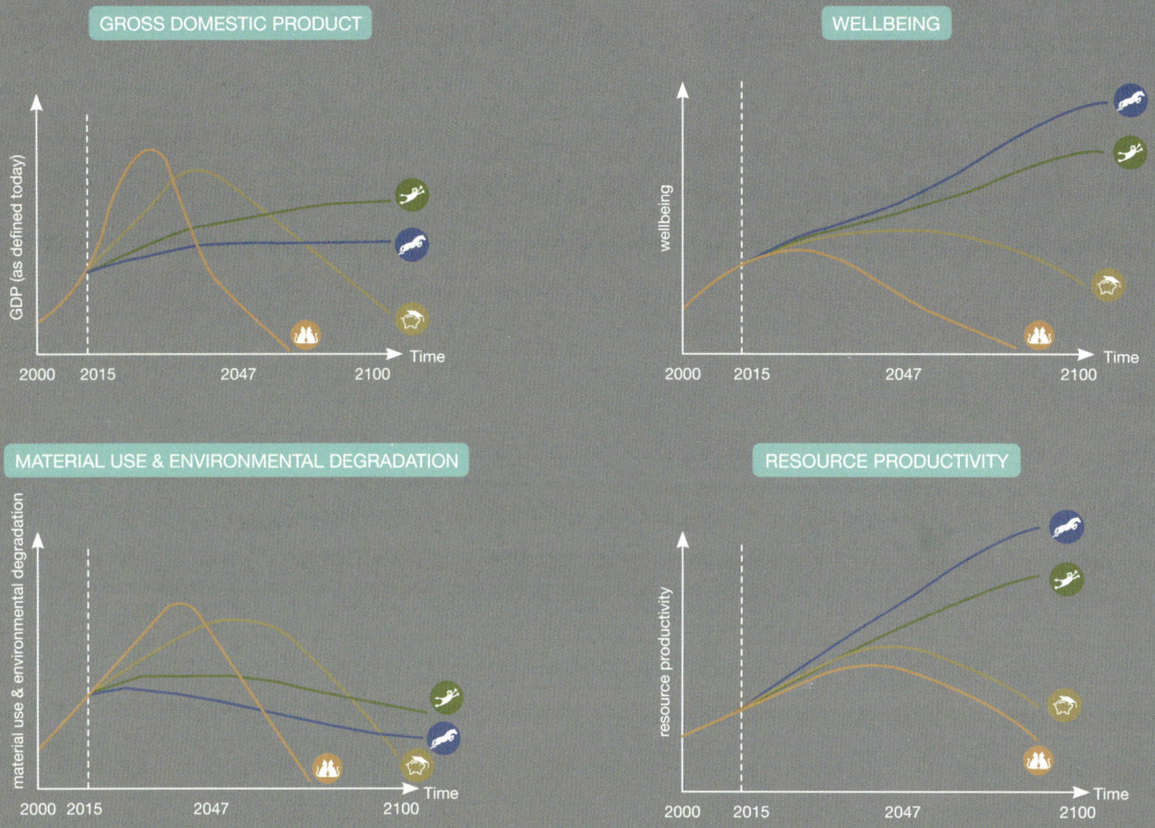

Current best knowledge indicates that the 21st Century is a period of profound change, of historical discontinuity when the future of humanity will be fundamentally determined by the choices we make today. Never before in human history have the critical elements of demography, economics, ecology, natural resources, technology and geopolitics come together into such a "perfect storm" of explosive confrontation with the imperatives of civilizational survival.

Given its size and population, India's future is closely linked, in both directions, with that of the world. Though this book focuses primarily on India, many of its insights apply, pari passu, to other developing countries and, indeed, to the world as a whole.

These charts attempt to show indicative trajectories of major indicators of progress. They are based on guesstimates of how the economic, social and natural processes would roll out over the coming century for each of the scenarios – Copycat, Piggyback,

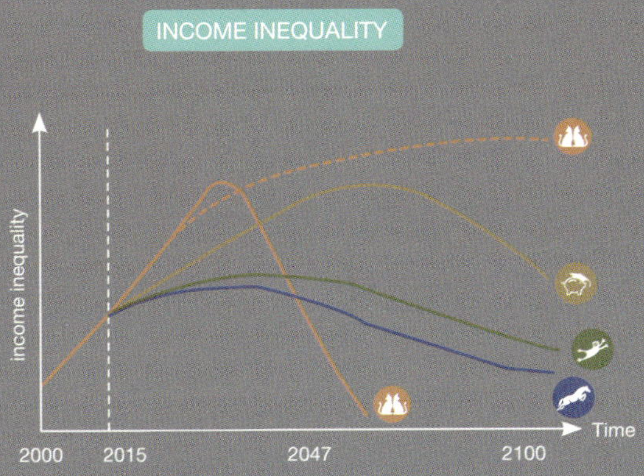

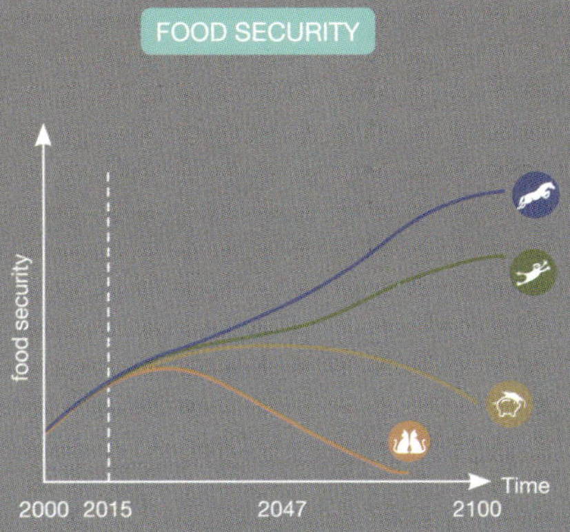

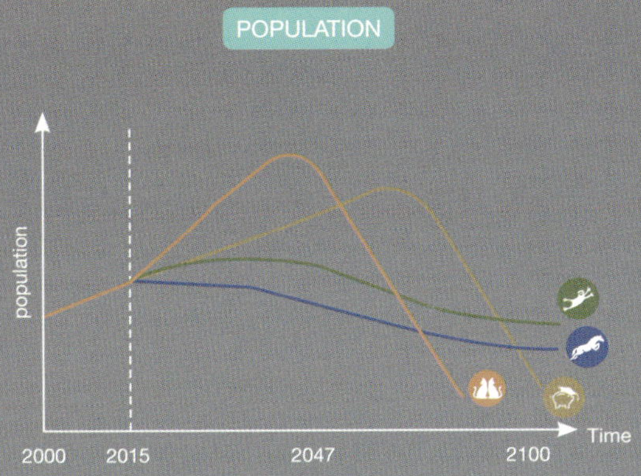

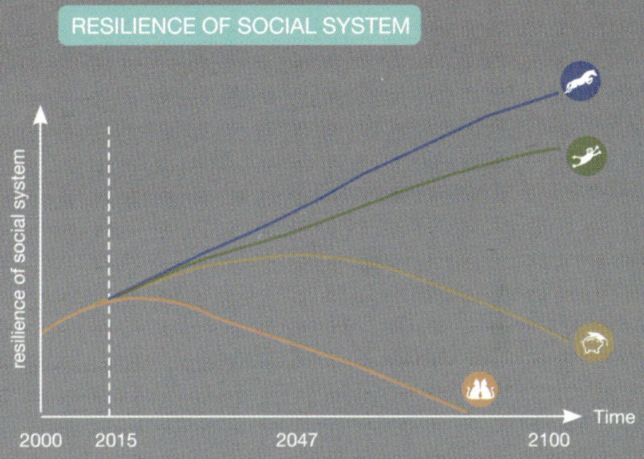

Leapfrog and Horsejump – in the context of India. Their purpose is to highlight the general patterns of how our future would unfold, depending on what choices we make today.

These charts are neither forecasts nor predictions. Their purpose is simply to present a broad picture that can help decision makers and the public imagine more clearly the futures that are likely for different development choices. They can hopefully facilitate thinking by them on the trade-offs that need to be managed for making India a good home for present and future generations. All the charts are drawn on the assumption that whatever scenario is chosen, the commitment to it would be complete and would be made today. If it is only partial or is delayed, the appropriate lag times and dilutions would displace the respective curves to the right and downwards. While the relative positioning of the curves in each chart is generally meaningful, their absolute positioning is NOT to scale.

04

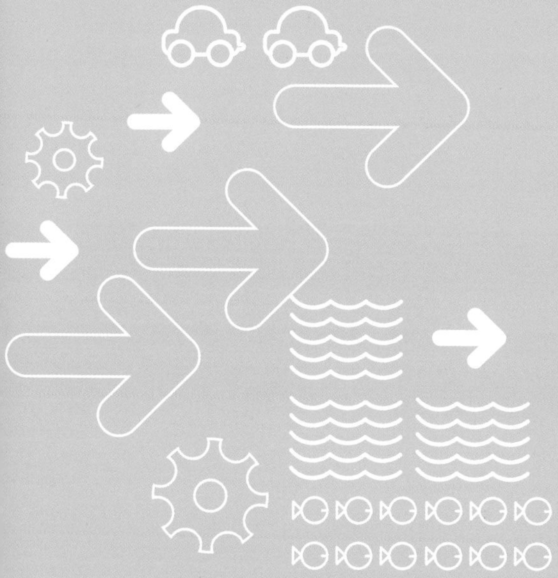

TRANSITIONS

for a Sustainable Future

The future is ours to choose

- How do we build a sustainable future for India?
- The Top Priorities for a Sustainable India
- Case studies

The best way to predict the future is to create it

ANONYMOUS

TRANSITIONS FOR A SUSTAINABLE FUTURE

Vision into Action

Few in our country today would disagree that we need a change and some even feel that a transformation of a fundamental nature is needed; but to achieve such change, we must have a clear idea of the direction we should head for and of how our huge ship of state can be reoriented towards it.

The Central Question right now is: How do we build a sustainable future for India?

Sustainable development – in which the environment, social equity and empowerment are goals of equal importance with economic improvement – cannot be achieved by economic policies that only nurture big, centralised, transportation-intensive, energy-guzzling, and resource-wasting production systems. Our future cannot be created by narrowly conceived short-term interventions or by the kinds of misplaced subsidies, give-away approaches common in the many 'so called' poverty alleviation programmes.

Perhaps above all, sustainable development means building human capacities to enable people to make endogenous choices – their own choices, reflecting their own realities, aspirations and their knowledge of their resource endowment. It also means widespread access to education, enterprise and empowerment that helps people to find meaning and dignity in their lives. This translates into building the technical, managerial and financial skills of people, creating institutions of local governance capable of managing resources for the benefit of the community. It involves setting up robust decision support systems and strong public infrastructure – not just the big power stations, highway systems, airports and dams but also local, renewable based energy production in remote areas, rural roads, and universal connectivity. In addition to maintaining the social and natural resource base, it means energising people and communities and the development of a vibrant, alert, and capable civil society.

A sustainable development paradigm supports such a rich mix of considerations of which economic development is one aspect. It puts both human wellbeing and planetary health as the development focus, with economic processes reinforcing relationship among people, and between people and the natural environment. We need to reorganise the role of economic processes and growth with respect to maximising human and planetary wellbeing. Only a strong national commitment in the form of laws, regulations and investments to an economically, socially and ecologically sustainable future for our nation can ensure that economic progress is a means to that end and not an end in itself. Such a framework of sustainable development has governance systems that integrate the dimensions of economic, social and environmental

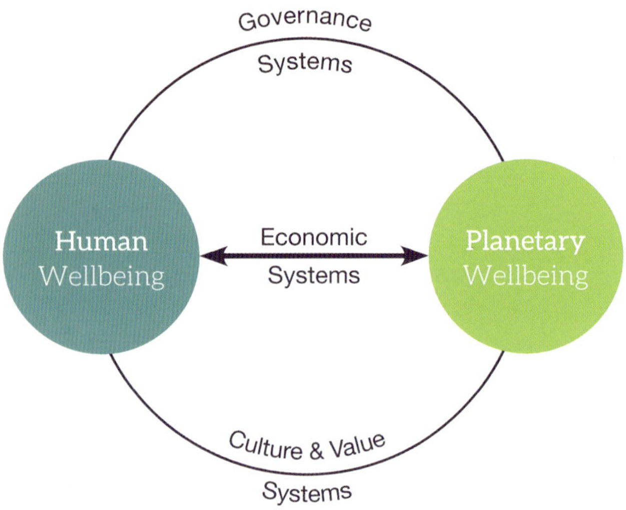

sustainability in policies and actions. It also defines a set of values and culture that are appropriate for each society to help guide its people in designing social systems and public institutions of governance needed to achieve the desired goals.

To create a sustainable future for India, each of us will have to evolve a better understanding of our long-term interest and all of us will have to work together-- locally, nationally and globally -- to make it possible. We will need systemic transformations at the level of both the ends (development outcomes) and the means (identifying risks; addressing root causes) and accelerating key drivers of change (for inclusive, resilient, and sustainable development). The transition implies a deep and structural (Leapfrog and Horsejump) changes in our – economic structures, society (collective set of values, norms, paradigms) and its practices (behaviours, implementation modalities) and governing institutions. Such a desirable change for a sustainable India, that ensures wellbeing for the people and planet, therefore, implies a fundamental transformation in our:

- **Social systems:** Alter values and lifestyles to embrace an acceptable minimum quality of life for all, peace and harmony in the community, and sustenance of the ecological systems that support us
- **Economic Systems:** Achieve green and inclusive economic growth and transform economic activity for sustainability
- **Governance Systems:** Develop participatory/inclusive, effective, forward looking, and legitimate systems

The Top Priorities for a Sustainable India

The social, economic, and governance transformations we need are overlapping and strongly interdependent. Taken together, they comprise a vision for achieving a sustainable future for all. In one sense this is a highly complex business and will therefore require a highly complex response. For the transitions to be effective, they must be systemic, so they must match, in character and complexity, the nature of the problems they seek to solve. By setting self-organising systems in motion, with appropriate and well-defined rules, it is possible for a simply stated solution to acquire the requisite variety to match the complexity of the problem. However, by breaking the complexity up into manageable action parts, it can be made more practical and tractable.

If there is a one-point agenda for sustainable development in India, it is the large-scale introduction of sustainable livelihoods. In the simplest terms, sustainable livelihoods are jobs. These jobs do, however, have a combination of attributes that set them apart from other, more common types of employment: they produce goods and services for local markets, particularly aimed at basic human needs; they generate a living income and thus purchasing power; and they help to regenerate the environmental resource base. The existence of sustainable livelihoods enhances the productive capabilities of people while boosting their self-esteem and social status, reducing unrest and laying the foundation of growing prosperity and social contribution. They provide a powerful synthesising, unifying concept that can bring the most disparate interests together to design more viable economic systems for the future in any country, rich or poor. By their very nature, sustainable livelihoods bind people to their communities and to their land, creating a symbiosis with these support systems. Not only do they thus have a positive impact on health, fertility reduction, migration, and other demographic behaviour, but they also permit a far more effective use of resources for the benefit of all. Sustainable livelihoods increases the capacities of people and communities to better adapt and build resilience towards change.

Livelihoods and lifestyles are inextricably linked. Simplistic theories on how the corporate sector is creating a new market for its products by redesigning, re-costing, and re-packaging them to suit the tastes and expectations of the poor at the 'bottom of the pyramid' miss the point that people must have the interest and the disposable income to be able to buy these products. In today's economy, purchasing power among the poor comes from income and income comes largely from taking part in the production process – unless job opportunities are created at the same time as the products, there can be neither buyers nor sellers for long.

The creation of sustainable livelihoods is relevant as it ensures that India's largest asset – its demographic advantage – does not become a liability. The constant highlighting of the youth as demographic dividend hides serious concerns of providing employment and food security for the future of our country.

We need to set in place a virtuous system that will enable the creation of sustainable livelihoods at scale – both as an ends and a means to achieve overall wellbeing. Based on our experience and expertise, we identify nine priorities, pivoted on the Basic Framework of Sustainable Development. These nine instruments can create the desired self-propelling processes and ripple effects to transform our vision into reality.

1. Invest in Systems and Institutions that Deliver Basic Needs Effectively and Universally
2. Invest in the Capacities of People to Participate Meaningfully in the Economy
3. Invest in Local Micro, Mini and Small Social Enterprises as Job-Creation Engines
4. Invest in Natural Capital
5. Encourage Sustainable Production through Sustainable Technologies
6. Promote Sustainable Lives and Lifestyles
7. Shift to Dynamic Planning and Green Infrastructure for Sustainable, Humane Settlements
8. Move from Shareholder to Stakeholder Businesses
9. Strengthen Local Government and Civil Society for Community Empowerment

PRIORITY 1

Invest in Systems and Institutions that Deliver Basic Needs Effectively and Universally

In the run up to 100 years as an independent nation, it is intolerable that India still has even one citizen who is impoverished, let alone the more than 600 million of its citizens who currently live in various degrees of deprivation. We must now change those aspects of our culture and economic policies that encourage excessive material consumption by some while accepting rampant unfulfilled need for most.

As the first step to a sustainable future, India needs to ensure that all its citizens have access to the means of satisfying their basic needs – food, water and sanitation, housing, energy, education and health care through solutions that minimise material use. The argument for provision of basic needs is self-evident. It is the first step before progressing on to meet higher-level human needs. For this, governments and civil society have to work together or separately to help build the confidence and capacity of individuals to lead a dignified life.

To achieve this goal, the country will need to:

- Promote and help finance decentralised service models and local enterprises that cater to the needs of all, especially the poor
- Enable everyone to access affordable education, health and hygiene and to make informed choices
- Enhance the effectiveness and efficiency of publicly provided services through development of fair partnership models involving public, private, civil, and community collaboration
- Encourage the application of sustainable mechanisms for basic needs provision such as climate smart agriculture, renewable energy and electrification, and green construction materials

"Decentralised delivery of basic needs, goods and services offers many opportunities while leaping over current challenges in interesting ways. It builds local capacities to service local markets and communities' creating more jobs, it reduces the risk of locking in capital that may be based on obsolete and potentially unsustainable large infrastructure enabling the system to quickly modernise as opportunities become available, and it provides an amazing opportunity to select and promote cleaner and greener technologies relevant to individual context." ZEENAT NIAZI

impact

- 1000 households electrified
- INR 156,500,000 invested in local economic development through partnerships
- 25 enterprises and 400 shops in backward regions linked with power plants
- 19,341 tonnes of carbon emissions saved

Renewable energy based service and delivery models for electrification - Smart Power for Environmentally-sound Economic Development (SPEED)

Uttar Pradesh, Madhya Pradesh, Bihar, Jharkhand and Chhattisgarh, India

In India, 40,000 villages are either un-electrified or de-electrified and over 400 million people do not have access to electricity. This lack of access to modern energy services has staggering consequences to achieve universal social and economic development. The Development Alternatives Group, through various initiatives have created a package of solutions for such village communities to secure their household and community energy needs by using renewable energy models.

The SPEED model of renewable energy based electrification, initiated in 2011, develops business models and implementation plans that deliver electricity from renewable sources through mini grids in energy deficient regions, enabling the electrification of households and creation of economic opportunity in India's most backward regions. In Rampura, a village in Bundelkhand, this set up has enabled the uninterrupted electricity supply for households for a fee, enabling for the first time after 60 years of independence, for village families to light up homes at night and for children to access computer based education.

A breakthrough in the SPEED initiative has been leveraging private capital from Energy Supply Companies to service power needs in electricity-starved regions through cleaner power infrastructure. It engages an ecosystem of stakeholders like industry and civil society to create financing and implementation models, for energy production and supply while minimising carbon footprint. The decentralised system increases efficiencies in management and reduces risks creating a compelling environment for accelerated action and sustained impact in the area of clean energy led economic development.

impact

- 120 artisans trained on eco - construction
- 18,000 green and skilled workdays created per year
- 500 houses and structures constructed

Artisan's Cooperative providing green construction services for affordable housing - Karigar Mandal

Madhya Pradesh, India

The rural housing deficit of 40 million units presents an opportunity to create jobs at scale. However, this opportunity may soon fracture the ecological capacity through the stresses the construction sector creates on natural resources and energy. Construction is recognised as the second highest contributor to green house gas emissions after the energy sector in India.

In rural parts of India, an artisan plays the role of mason, architect and contractor for providing housing solutions. The artisan is responsible for all choices made in terms of the material resources used in construction. Hence, it is imperative to ensure that these choices are influenced by appropriate knowledge and available technologies.

Karigar Mandal is a social enterprise, incubated by Development Alternatives in 2008, that builds capacities of masons through dissemination of sustainable eco-friendly construction techniques. Registered as a Mutually Aided Cooperative Society (MACS) with the Madhya Pradesh State Government in India, Karigar Mandal facilitates creation of eco-houses by acting as a service provider to provide construction services and training masons to fulfill the needs of the people while contributing to low carbon development. The masons under the Karigar Mandal, help meet the growing demand for rural housing while minimising environmental degredation.

The availability of skilled masons enables new homeowners to make informed and empowered choices. A frontrunner of green job creation - Karigar Mandal has supported training of artisans across the state of Madhya Pradesh to service their social housing initiative. The Karigar Mandal model has a large potential for replication by skill enhancement and currently six other Karigar Mandals are being developed in the Bundelkhand Region.

PRIORITY 2

Invest in the Capacities of People to Participate Meaningfully in the Economy

People need help to acquire the capacity to adopt sustainable lifestyles and livelihoods to enable them to stand on their feet and contribute to building the nation, while coping with the stresses and shocks that are common in a country in transition. Simply defined, "Capacity" enables people to have the ability, backed by the decision systems and infrastructures they need, to identify, formulate, and analyse the problems of high relevance to their societies and design effective strategies to solve them. The access to knowledge and capacity allows communities to choose from among different technology and livelihoods options and adopt those most appropriate for local markets and conditions. Capacity also enables societies to implement solutions and learn lessons from experience so as to redesign future solutions even more effectively. Women need to be at the center of capacity building initiatives as they play a critical role in sustainable development.

To be effective, such capacity needs to be built up in all sectors and levels of society – government, business, academia, media, and civil society at the national, provincial, and local levels – with opportunities for strong collaborative experiences leading to a tradition of dynamic interaction among them.

To enable the capacities of people for sustainable livelihoods, India must:

- Adopt new innovative systems for basic education and skill development as well as improve learning outcomes that are necessary for livelihoods and entrepreneurship
- Improve access to quality education services and infrastructure
- Enable members of all communities to access fair credit services
- Create local knowledge centres that promote entrepreneurship and information for improved access to livelihoods and the productivity potential of communities
- Invest in capacities of the marginalised, especially women

"If we want to help poor people out, one way to do that is to help them explore and use their own capability. Human being is full of capacity, full of capability, is a wonderful creation. But many people never get a chance to explore that, never."

MUHAMMAD YUNUS

impact

- 120,000 women functionally literate
- 60 enterprises developed and 200 women provided employment
- 1,300 women provided with skill development training

Innovative learning systems for economic empowerment of women - Literacy to Self-Reliance

Uttar Pradesh, Madhya Pradesh, Bihar, Jharkand, Haryana, Delhi NCR, Uttarakhand and Rajasthan, India

India is home to 40 per cent of the world's illiterate - of which two-thirds are women. The lack of literacy and capacity adversely impacts their ability to access basic rights and entitlements, undertake economic activities or participate in the decision making of their homes and community.

Development Alternatives has initiated an end-to-end solution for women through its 'Literacy to Self-Reliance' programme. Women, in this initiative, are first provided with functional literacy and consequently undergo training aimed at enhancing their vocational skills and confidence to undertake income generation activities. Trainings for personality development and knowledge on health, hygiene and related aspects are also conducted.

Functional literacy, i.e., to be able to read, write and perform basic mathematics is provided by the ICT based programme 'TARA Akshar+'. This is a unique computer-based teaching innovation that uses advanced teaching techniques and enables a learner to master the art of reading and writing in Hindi and do simple calculations within 56 days and at very low cost. The use of advanced cognitive innovations that include strong learning and reinforcement aids, advanced memory enhancing techniques and effective methods ensures a 92% success rate. Post basic literacy, life skill training is imparted through TARA Livelihood Academy - the skill development arm of Development Alternatives. Vocational, employability or entrepreneurship skills are imparted to the women over a period of two months based on the results of a training needs assessment. TARA Livelihood Academy acts as a facilitator in placements and business set up for these women and further acquaints them to existing industry and market trends.

The 'Literacy to Self-Reliance' programme has enabled women to become successful entrepreneurs and leaders in their communities. While many of them have become tailors, beauticians, and grocery shop owners; a few have been elected as members of the local government bodies.

impact

- 23,000 doctors from 83 low income countries in the Americas, Africa and Asia and several thousand more are in the pipeline
- Enrollment from 123 nations with representation from over 100 ethnic groups who will benefit from the new MDs upon graduation

Photo Credit: Latin Post

Quality healthcare to the underserved
- Latin American School of Medicine, *Cuba*

Good healthcare is a universal right, but millions of people do not have regular access to a family doctor. A large number of communities do not have physicians in their neighbourhoods and lack reliable means of transportation to get to the nearest doctor. Besides the dearth of doctors, recent studies find that in many cases, minority communities who do manage to find a doctor are not given the same level of medical attention as their well-off counterparts.

The Latin American School of Medicine (ELAM), Cuba was established in 2005 by the Cuban government to build capacity of the communities to be able to access quality healthcare in areas where few good doctors were willing to go. The school recruits students from around the world coming from the remotest villages and poverty-stricken slums in their countries, and provides them with a world-class education in medicine under a full scholarship. This is in exchange for a pledge that they will practice where most doctors don't - in poor and underserved communities upon graduation. The hope is that they will help transform access to care, the health picture in impoverished areas, and even the way medicine itself is learned and practiced, and that they will become pioneers in our global reach for universal health coverage.

Preference is given to applicants who are financially needy or from marginalised communities who show the most commitment to returning to practice in their poor communities. In addition to free tuition and accommodation, a small stipend is provided to the students. The unique and holistic pedagogy with a focus of team-based approach ensures the development of competent doctors to deal with all issues related to public health improvement where it is needed the most.

Today, ELAM is the largest schools of medicine in the world by enrollment. Approximately 20,000 students from 110 countries were enrolled in ELAM in 2013. Tackling the problem of the concentration of the health workforce in the cities and the private sector, these students will return to their underserved hometowns to practice, and thereby help strengthen the health of the population in poor countries.

PRIORITY 3

Invest in Local Micro, Mini and Small Social Enterprises as Job-Creation Engines

Jobs are, of course, the most basic need of all. If one has a job, one has income and with an adequate income, one can take care of all other basic needs. With growing mechanisation, the capacity of agriculture to absorb additional labour is rapidly diminishing. The rapid mechanisation of industry and the financial and marketing imperatives of the global economy, are leading even faster to jobless growth in the corporate sector. With other formal sectors like governments cutting back on their payrolls gradually and civil society not having the resources to provide large numbers of jobs, it is only the medium, small and – mostly – the mini and micro enterprises that are able to provide opportunities for work to the growing workforce.

Micro, small and medium enterprises are market-based, profit-making businesses that are mostly small and generally local. In India, as in most economies, they happen to be the largest generators of jobs and livelihoods. To be economically viable, they need to operate under substantially modified market mechanisms that help them become competitive. To be socially sustainable, they must work with full-cost accounting and also generate positive social impacts. This will not only create jobs but also boost local economies leading to equitable growth and economic diversity. Social enterprises that integrate considerations not only of economic efficiency but also of environmental soundness and social equity into business decisions need to be nurtured and incentivised.

To boost local micro, mini and small social enterprises, India has to:

- Promote entrepreneurship through the formal education curriculum
- Boost job creating sectors such as the manufacturing and construction
- Facilitate development of enterprises by streamlining administrative burdens and providing critical infrastructure
- Design and promote mechanisms that will create and service green SMEs with necessary technical support, financial linkages and marketing support
- Promote decentralised/ regional industrial hubs and centres to boost local economies of scale
- Set in place policies that will direct investments into these green micro, small and medium enterprises
- Establish procurement policies that support social enterprises

"Without any vision of transformation in productive structure and the upgrading of the productive capabilities that make it possible, the vision of development...can only be described as development without development" HA-JOON CHANG

impact

- 1,000+ green building enterprises created
- INR 6,000 million revenue generated by green building enterprises
- 300,000 households access safe eco-housing and sanitation

Incubating business models for micro and small enterprise development

Technology and Action for Rural Advancement (TARA), *India*

Technology and Action for Rural Advancement (TARA), a social enterprise of the Development Alternatives Group, develops and promotes scalable solutions for people and our planet. It incubates enterprise packages and business models for take up by aspiring micro and small entrepreneurs. These models are designed to promote low carbon pathways and inclusive growth through enterprise development in the sector of rural housing, renewable energy, water management, sustainable agriculture, waste management and recycling.

These solutions are multiplied for scale through various TARA partners and TARA incubated companies for maximum impact. TARA with its partners have facilitated the establishment of more than thousand enterprises since its inception, to inspire local economies and create green jobs. Services are provided to entrepreneurs in the form of technology, finance, business management and marketing support. Contemporary in nature, these business solutions are attuned to be responsive to the dynamic nature of the market, integrated with the dimensions of environmental sustainability, technological innovations and changing labour markets.

As a result of TARA's efforts over the past two decades, a wide variety of basic needs products for water purification, clean cooking, solar lighting, construction have been made available in the rural market through local enterprises. For example, close to a 100 million Micro Concrete Roofing (MCR) tiles have been sold, sufficient to cover more than 200,000 village houses. Some of TARA's technologies, such as machines to make bricks using fly ash, a major waste from coal-fired power plants, have now become mainstream products for the construction sector.

impact

- 109 innovators
- INR 76 million invested in seed funding
- Investments worth INR 1,124 million raised
- 15 million lives impacted

Photo Credit: Villgro

Creating successful innovative enterprises that impact the lives of the poor – Villgro, *India*

Villgro funds and incubates early stage, innovation-based social enterprises that impact the lives of India's poor in the areas of healthcare, education, agri-business, energy among others. Villgro supports innovative ideas by providing mentorship, talent, funds and networks to social enterprises. The team assists early-stage social entrepreneurs as they tackle their most pressing business challenges ranging from raising finance for their enterprises to solidifying their business models.

Villgro invests through equity and/or quasi-equity in enterprises at various stages of their startup journey - from prototyping to when they are developing their business model to a stage of early growth in the business. It exits once the business is investable and ready to scale. Typically, Villgro stays invested in a company for three to four years and if the company hits certain milestones, it can fund them with up to Rs. 65 lakhs over this time.

In order to address the talent gap in its portfolio enterprises, the Villgro Fellowship programme recruits and places mid-career professionals in these social enterprises for a period of one year, during which time they contribute their skills and knowledge to addressing key issues in these enterprises. In turn, Villgro Fellows are exposed to a start-up working environment and the social enterprise ecosystem. The organisation also creates investment, knowledge and network partnerships for its entrepreneurs. Its unconventional platform seeks to take the social enterprise movement across India and nurture entrepreneurs through events that showcase initiatives, share expert knowledge from sector leaders and connect entrepreneurs to an extended network of ideas, resources and opportunities.

Since its inception in 2001, Villgro has helped launch and develop successful business initiatives like Biosense, Promethean Power Systems, Skymet, Under the Mango Tree, Rope, Desicrew, and Sustaintech among others.

"In the past, reuse and service-life extension were often strategies in situations of scarcity or poverty.... Today, they are signs of good resource husbandry and smart management"

WALTER STAHEL

PRIORITY 4

Invest in natural capital

The health of the ecosystem is of intrinsic importance to every single citizen as they depend directly and indirectly on the services it provides to the national economy. For the 50 percent of the people in India, whose livelihoods are in direct daily contact with nature, their protection is a matter of fundamental rights. Investing in natural capital, thus, represents an important economic development strategy, a link not adequately recognised by India's existing development model. The current compartmentalised treatment is pushing India to choose between development and conservation of nature. The economic system has to be recognised as a sub-system of the people and nature (i.e., the social and environmental system).

The conventional linear take-make-discard economic model is falsely based on an assumption of unlimited supply of resources and energy and endless sinks to absorb wastes and emissions. There is growing evidence that there are several possibilities for producing higher economic growth using fewer materials and energy. One way is to decouple economic growth from natural resource use. This implies efficient use of natural resources in an equitable, secure and environmentally benign manner for human wellbeing. However, this is not enough, given the massive destruction of nature that has already taken place. The natural capital base will also need to be restored and regenerated and the operating system of the economy will have to be transformed. This can be facilitated through investments in infrastructure, programmes and circular economy approaches that enhance the natural resource base. Lessons and insights from how living systems manage to be productive and produce no wastes are relevant to designing technologies and economies that work more optimally than today's highly compartmentalised ones.

For such sustainable resource management, India needs to:

- Redirect investment into nature to enhance natural resources such as land and water systems
- Incentivise businesses to adopt cradle to cradle and waste to wealth approaches
- Put the responsibility of cleaning up on the polluter
- Adopt the precautionary approach and choose solutions with minimum risk of causing damage
- Create fiscal instruments and incentives that make green economic activity attractive
- Create standards based on triple bottom line sustainability goals
- Use public procurement practices to accelerate demand for green goods and services
- Ensure valuation of ecosystem services through adoption of full cost accounting systems
- Adopt zero waste strategies in all manufacturing and services delivery
- Adopt zero waste strategies in all manufacturing and services delivery

impact

- More than 200 check-dams established since 1982
- Appx. 600 million litres of water harvested each year
- 50% of land under single cropping converted to double cropping
- 25% increase in agricultural productivity and farmer income

Restoring ecosystem services for a water secure future – Check-dams

Madhya Pradesh and Uttar Pradesh, India

Over the last two decades, ground water levels have been falling at an alarming rate across India. This may largely be attributed to the over-extraction of ground water for intensive agriculture coupled with a reduction in recharge potential due to deforestation and other land use changes. With ground water stores collapsing, and rainfall patterns becoming increasingly erratic, agriculture, especially in rain-fed areas, has been severely compromised. Falling crop production and abandoned farms owing to lack of water has been forcing large numbers of farmers into migration, penury, debt and even suicide besides undermining the food security of the country.

In response to the chronic drought situation in Bundelkhand, Development Alternatives pioneered the establishment of check-dams as a low cost and sustainable technology for realising water security outcomes. Besides fulfilling its core mandate of water security, the check-dam technology has amply demonstrated its catalytic multi-dimensional impacts in regenerating ecosystem services such as soil nutrient recycling, flood and erosion control, restoring the productive potential of land. This has also generated livelihood and income opportunities and promoted equitable socio-economic development.

Enhanced water security effectively lays the foundation for sustainable and climate resilient agricultural development and diversification that can in turn be leveraged for developing farm and off-farm enterprises that energise the local economy. Farmers are supported in developing and adopting climate resilient and sustainable agriculture models and techniques. Small farmers in the vicinity are encouraged to adopt agri-horti models in their barren lands based on the principles of agroforestry that ensures livelihood and nutritional security as well as reclamation of degraded land in the area An analysis shows that a check-dam leads on average to 50 per cent increase in cropping intensity and 25 per cent increase in productivity and income for farmers in the location, making the initial investment completely recoverable within the first 2-3 years of the intervention.

DA promotes a community based participatory approach for the establishment and maintenance of these check-dams, ensuring that benefits are long term and equitably distributed while also inculcating appreciation and stewardship of ecosystem services amongst the community. The check-dam technology has been widely adopted by other development organisations and the Government for large-scale implementation across the country.

impact

- Nearly 20,000 acres of tropical desert like savannah is reforested.
- The forestation of 8,000 HA has resulted in 10 percent more precipitation.
- It is a self-sufficient society, as the community is food and water sovereign and generates its own energy and fuel.

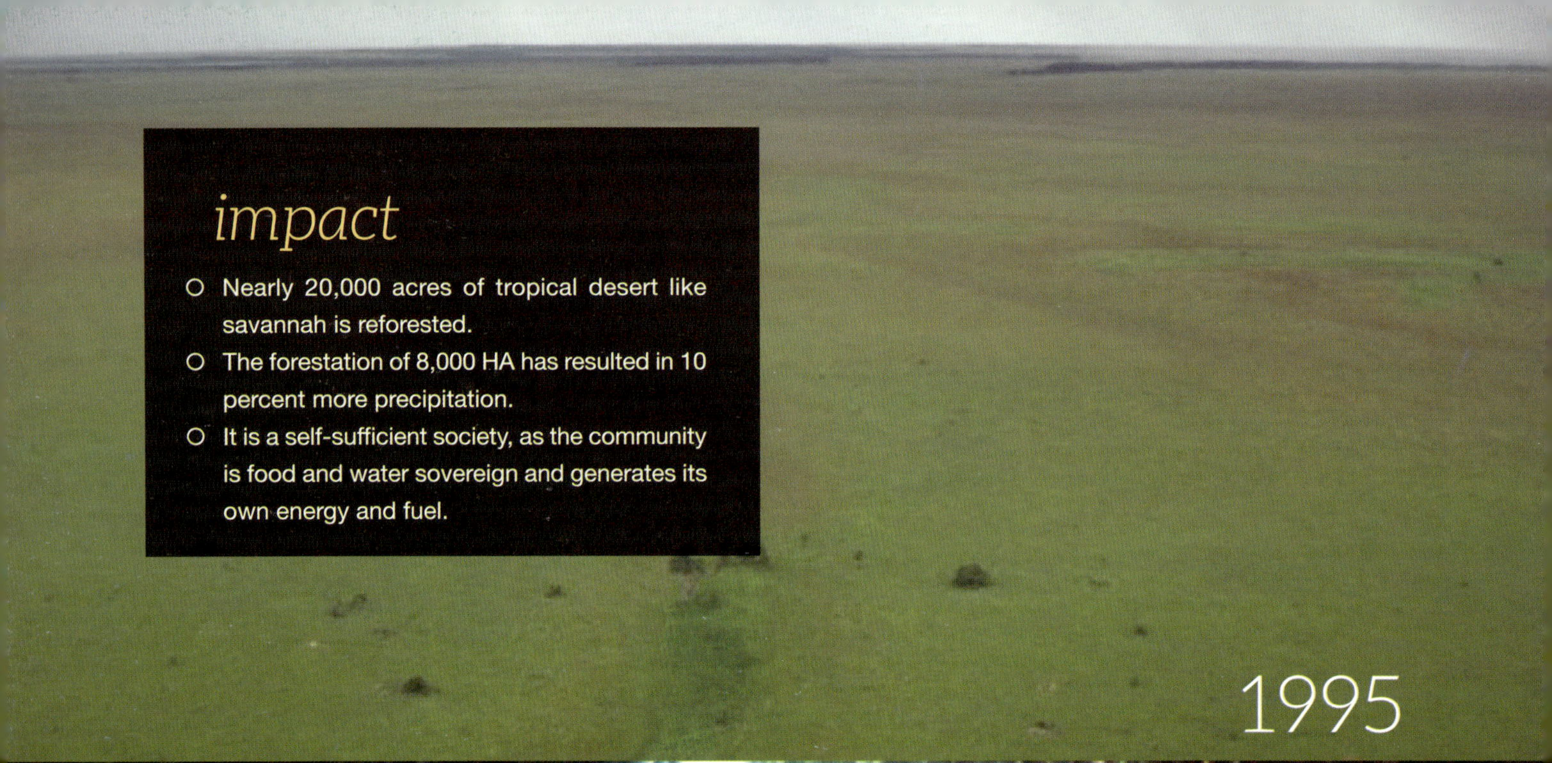

Photo Credit: Zero Emissions Research and Initiatives

From barren savannah to a sustainable society - Las Gaviotas

Vichada, Colombia

Las Gaviotas demonstrates that it is possible to convert deserted barren savannah into a sustainable society, which is a luxurious oasis of peace, by investing in nature. Pioneered by Paolo Lugari in 1984, this initiative began with the planting of Caribbean pine trees with the innovative use of mycorrhizal fungi that acted as saliva for the trees in the highly acidic and inhospitable soil. The success of this regenerated area enabled the initiation of economic activities and validated that carbon sinks unleash a chain reaction of positive effects.

The pine trees provided the shade for indigenous flora and fauna to revive and thrive. Over the years, this forest has expanded to approximately 20,000 acres with biodiversity of 250 tropical flora. The presence of the forest altered the local climate by increasing the rainfall by 10 percent, converting Las Gaviotas into a net supplier of drinking water, supporting its successful crystalline water bottling initiative. The abundance of water is a byproduct of the emerging forest.

The Gaviotans furthered their economic initiatives with the discovery that their pine forest can produce twice as much resin as any other resin-tapping forest in the world using an enzyme beneficial for the trees, contrary to conventional practice of using sulphuric acid. The Gaviotans produce a very high-grade resin which is converted to colofonia (used in paper and paint industry) in their resource efficient and zero-waste facility.

All energy requirements are met from innovative and creative renewable energy technologies. The community is generating power with turbine engines fueled by the aging pines in their forest. The pine tree plantation is complemented with the development palm trees that support the production of biodiesel for the trucks that transport their products to Bogota.

Las Gaviotas is now a self-sustaining community. It supports approximately 2,000 people through jobs. Water, tree resins, and biofuels are all harvested for cash flow. The people garner health benefits from regular exercise (all transport is on bicycles) and everyone receives free drinking water. Housing, health care, energy provision, livelihood, and food security are all positively impacted by the development at Las Gaviotas, which has increased the social capital. It has become a center of creativity, where innovations are driven by the meticulous observation of natural phenomena, and the self-confidence in the search for local solutions for local problems. If this model were applied to the 200 million acres under consideration in Venezuela, Brazil, and Peru, it could generate 15 million jobs while capturing the annual equivalent of Japan's carbon emissions.

"The choices.....India make[s] in the next few years will lead the world either towards a future beset by growing ecological and political instability - or down a development path based on efficient technologies and better stewardship of resources"

Worldwatch Institute 'State of the World 2006

PRIORITY 5

Encourage sustainable production through sustainable technologies

Many contemporary economies have demonstrated the central role of technology in human progress. Their experience has, however, shown the critical need for care in selection of the types of technology, to avoid wholesale destruction of human, social and environmental values. It has become clear that how something is produced, where it is produced and for whom it is produced are issues as important as what is produced and by whom. Technology that serves the long-term goals of human development while minimising the use of non-regenerating resources is defined as 'sustainable technology'.

Sustainable technology usually springs best from endogenous creativity, in response to local needs and possibilities. Relevant for use by the common people, it aims directly to improve the quality of their lives, using the physical potential of an area while maintaining harmony between people and nature. It derives maximum leverage from the local cultural environment by drawing upon existing managerial and technical skills and providing the basis for extending them. Sustainable technology often combines modern science and traditional knowledge: a method, a process, a design, a device or a product, which will open up new possibilities and potential for improving the quality of life. It requires frameworks for innovation and delivery very different from those that exist today, either in the global economy or in the village.

With the evolution of societal perceptions, aspirations and conditions, and with recent developments in science, design, new materials and production processes, a spurt in technology innovation is critical for solving the problems of poverty. New products and technologies, many with significant, positive social and environmental spin-offs, are now possible for mass distribution as a result of the application of sophisticated scientific and technological knowledge.

Recommendations for India to boost sustainable technology development and uptake are:

- Select appropriate technology such that it satisfies the needs of the end client and successfully and takes advantage of the opportunities and constraints of the production and marketing processes
- Design technologies that can reconcile the conflicting requirements of the market, nature and people – needing systems for innovation and delivery of the highest sophistication
- Incentivise innovation that reduce the use of critical and scarce resources such as soil, water and fossil fuels
- Encourage industries and consumers to recycle, reuse and reduce use of resources
- Adopt fiscal and monetary incentives for adoption of sustainable technologies
- Ensure strict regulatory frameworks that favour green and disincentivise brown technologies

impact

- 230 million fly ash bricks, 9 million roof tiles and 21 million floor tiles and pavers made available
- Production of over INR 1,500 million worth of goods, with contribution to the local economy of over INR 960 million
- Over 2,000 persons provided employment directly, with over 5,000 additionally employed indirectly.
- Besides the jobs in production, over 1,000 local masons have been trained who are using their skills to service rural families.

Greening the construction sector through sustainable technology development – Brick Sector

Rapidly growing economies like ours rely on the infrastructure and construction sectors to fuel growth. Bricks form the backbone of these sectors. However, brick production in India, with emissions estimated at 150 million tonnes CO_2 every year, is deemed as the single largest source of air pollution, exerting a high pressure on natural resources like soil and coal. In addition to the environmental impact, there are serious social implications such as the unsanitary and hazardous working conditions of labour.

Development Alternatives has pioneered the innovation and large scale accelerated adoption of sustainable brick production technologies that improve overall energy efficiency and reduction of emissions – Compressed Stabilised Earth Blocks, Fly Ash Bricks and Eco Kilns. The TARA Eco-kiln technology (based on Vertical Shaft Brick Kiln process) has resulted in significant coal savings ranging between 30 to 40 per cent per year. Emissions of SO_2, NO_x and CO_2 are well below the norms prescribed for conventional kilns and overall wastages are reduced due to inherent properties of the technology and improved firing practices. Fly Ash Brick technology meets the dual challenge of meeting the increasing brick deficit while utilising in large amounts the industrial waste generated by power plants. The stabilised compressed earth block technology uses non-agricultural soil with less than 10 per cent addition of a binder such as cement to form bricks that give strengths of equivalent to class A, and can be used in a variety of structures. The technology uses minimal energy; small-scale production can be done with human energy and results in negligible emissions only those attributable to the binder. Thus, it is amongst the most eco-friendly materials for construction.

These technologies lend themselves to various scales of production and application due to their modular nature. They are adopted by small-scale enterprises that require small capital investments with quick turn over rates making them attractive to new and existing entrepreneurs. Creating localised green and dignified jobs, the availability of these technologies enables enterprises to utilise local resources to service local demands.

Development Alternatives' role in promoting the use and influencing state and national level regulatory policies to promote sustainable production has led to the establishment of over 800 sustainable technology based brick production units in Bihar, Madhya Pradesh, Orissa and Maharashtra. In addition, these technologies are being transferred to other countries in Asia and Africa like Vietnam, Pakistan, Nepal, Bangladesh, South Africa and Malawi.

impact

- Eastgate's ventilation system costs one-tenth that of a comparable air-conditioned building and uses 35 per cent less energy than comparable conventional buildings in Harare.
- In the building's first five years, its unique design saved its owners $3.5 million in energy costs.

Photo Source: http://rdpauw.blogspot.in

Emulating termite based design systems for sustainable development - Eastgate Centre

Harare, Zimbabwe

The world is developing economically at a rapid rate and without intending to, the implications of which have created sustainability problems. Fortunately, solutions to these can be adapted from the time-tested patterns and strategies of nature available to us, to combat some of the challenges we face today.

The Eastgate Centre in Harare, Zimbabwe, designed by Mick Pearce in the 1990s, based on the principles of biomimicry, illustrates one of the best green architecture buildings and ecologically sensitive adaptations.

In a country like Zimbabwe, where the weather varies dramatically between summer and winter, maintaining comfortable temperatures of conventional glass buildings is extremely costly and inefficient. In such buildings air conditioning technologies continuously recycle air to retain a controlled atmosphere, which is an expensive, inefficient and polluting system.

Alternatively, in the Eastgate Centre, the technology used for ventilation in the building has been inspired from the way African termites construct their self-cooling nest. The Centre is ventilated entirely through natural mechanisms, with no conventional air-conditioning or heating, yet the temperatures in the building remain regulated all year round.

Corresponding to the central chimney of the termite mounds, the inside of the building has a seven-story, semi-protected atrium, surrounded by four heavy masonary walls on the exterior. The complex has two parallel buildings, separated by an open space, which is covered by glass but open to local breezes. Air is constantly drawn in from outside through several vents across the building and is warmed or cooled by the concrete structure depending on which is hotter. The naturally conditioned air is then channeled to various parts of the Eastgate Centre via ducts, before finally passing through the chimneys on the top. Fresh air pulled in replaces any stale air in the ducts. Outside of being eco-efficient and better for the environment, these savings also trickle down to the tenants whose rents are 20 percent lower than those of occupants in the surrounding buildings. The building is also rooted in local culture. With its heavy masonry walls on the exterior of the building, it is an expression of the traditional native stone masonry architecture from which Zimbabwe derives its name.

A number of problems related to sustainability that the world grapples with today, can be addressed by designing technologies that emulate the ways of nature, as illustrated through the design of the Eastegate Centre.

PRIORITY 6

Promote sustainable lives & lifestyles

We seem to be caught between two basic choices - either, we accept a future that is scarce and unsafe leading to wars over resources or we drastically cut the per capita use of materials and energy by adopting alternative lifestyles that can lead to universal human fulfilment, achieved within the planetary boundaries. In conforming to the principle of sufficiency whatever we consume and waste, we must not transgress the capacity of nature to rejuvenate itself on a continuing basis. This means that the prices and incentives that drive consumption behaviour have to be realigned to provide more equitable access to the goods and services on offer in the marketplace while promoting conservation of resources and the environment.

We should aim for convergence: everyone, and particularly over-consumers, must now reduce the material intensity of their lifestyles and under-consumers need to use what resources are necessary to improve their lives, until the two converge to an acceptable level that lies within the limits set by nature. Currently, the best estimates for this limit, per person averaged worldwide, appear to be six tonnes per year of material resources and about 3 Kilowatts of energy. Countries with high population growth like India should find ways to reduce that growth, particularly by pursuing the most effective deterrents to large families: education for girls and remunerative jobs for women. In parallel to this, we will need to find ways to achieve the desired level of human fulfilment through use of the highest efficiency technologies available.

It is this shift in our behaviour change that will ultimately positively influence societal consumption patterns and technological innovations that build local economies for inclusive growth.

For this, India will have to

- Provide hard and soft incentives to change consumer behaviour and shift material consumption to services such as sharing of underutilised assets and leasing of equipment
- Drive end user campaigns to increase awareness of smarter consumer choices
- Create knowledge and new narratives to influence values and mind-sets to consider green and local consumption as a desirable and responsible goal

> "It is not about consuming less but consuming better" UNEP

impact

- Doubled the green cover of Delhi, in partnership with the Government of Delhi
- 50,000 people benefit from the water conservation system advocated
- 126,000 students in Uttar Pradesh have gained access to safe drinking water though the water purification systems installed
- Pioneered the eco-festival concept to celebrate with eco-colours on Holi and and no toxic paints on Durga Puja and Diwali

Civil society for environment stewardship - Community Led Environment Action Network, India (CLEAN-India)

India is in the midst of rapid urbanisation. Owing to poor knowledge and lack of community action, communities in these upcoming towns and cities are either not aware of the environmental impacts or are unable to cope with these.

India is also one of the youngest countries in the world today, with more than half of its citizens below 35 years of age. Development Alternatives launched the CLEAN-India programme in 1996 in upcoming towns and cities to influence the mind space of the youth to become responsible decision makers for a sustainable tomorrow. It is a nationwide programme on environmental assessment, awareness, action and advocacy, promoting behaviour change amongst the youth with the vision of developing a greener future.

CLEAN-India raises awareness and provides practical solutions for issues like water quality and water management, sanitation, land use and urban biodiversity conservation, air quality, energy efficiency, waste management, carbon footprint reduction and actions to respond to climate change. The CLEAN India programme works on a 4A approach – Assessment, Awareness, Action, Advocacy. Assessment of the urban environmental issues in a participatory manner using scientific data and people's perceptions, Awareness about the problems in the city environment and possible solutions through campaigns, catalysing and supporting Action by school children and youth and Advocacy to mainstream the identified good practices and behaviours amongst city municipalities.

CLEAN-India has mobilised an extensive network of environmentally conscious citizens assuming responsibility and evolving solutions to problems, across the country. Besides the core network of 28 NGOs, 300 schools, 800 teachers, 60,000 trainer students and 1.25 million other students; several other citizens groups like resident welfare associations, parent forums, local business associations and clubs are increasingly participating actively in environmental improvement activities. It is also gaining traction in the international arena and has been designated the focal point for Earth Charter, India.

The CLEAN-India programme endeavours to galvanise a movement for a cleaner tomorrow, a movement that will reverberate throughout the society to lead sustainable lifestyles, a movement which will compel policy makers to create greener cities.

impact

- 1.5 million square feet of luxurious residential communities in Bangalore and Mysore
- Savings of at least 35,000-50,000 litres of water per home, with at least a 100,000 litres of water being harvested per year per home
- Fresh water needs brought down by at least 30%. Up to 60-70% savings on water bills
- Reduction in a third of energy consumption. Saving of 60-70% per month on electricity bills
- Close to 3 tons of wet waste managed locally
- Savings of at least 900-1100 tonnes of CO_2/annum on each project. Total Carbon Sequestration through various activities of approximately 136 tons/year

Photo Credit: ZED Homes

Living with sensibility and responsibility - ZED Homes

Bengaluru, Mysore, Chennai, India

ZED (Zero Energy Development) Homes, constructed by Biodiversity Conservation India Pvt. Ltd. (BCIL), are luxurious, green residential complexes in Chennai, Bangalore, and Mysore. In the Gandhain pursuit, ZED initiative is focused on sustainably creating zero energy homes. Every aspect of Zed is designed to conserve and reuse natural resources and to have minimal impact on the environment. These homes, use light weight concrete blocks instead of bricks that use precious top soil and require temperatures of over 400°C to bake and adopt. The building methods and methodologies save over 180 bags of cement and more than 20% on steel usage per home.

There is more than 50% independence from the grid for energy through management of demand side load with the set up low energy requirement systems to bring down consumption footprints. ACs that run on 5 amps (as opposed to 15A), use of plastering methods that help shield the home from heat ingress and the use of fans that only consume 28-30W are all factors that enable this without any compromise on comfort or aesthetics. Residents do not depend on the city for fresh water supply but manage their own fresh water and wastewater with minimal maintenance hassles, thereby reducing fresh water demand by 30%. Zero dependence on grid for water needs, low flow water fixtures, water recycling, development of ground water recharging and replenishing systems and water treatment that makes black water potable are adopted to minimise wastage and resource use.

Comprehensive waste segregation at source with wet waste being managed locally and non-biodegradable waste going only to identified recycling centers are services provided at ZED homes. Zero food miles programs to meet at least 20-30% of residents food needs locally, landscaping and gardening that has been done houses a large number of local biodiversity species. ZED's range of forest-free fully recyclable furniture is made from certified and sustainably harvested timber with no nails and brads. Joints are engineered to bond with wooden dowels and chemical-free bonding adhesives or any chemical processing.

Demonstrating a blend of luxury and environmental sustainability, profitability and effective resource management, and urban residential proliferation with energy conservation, BCIL has pioneered forward looking and path-breaking models to promote sustainable lifestyles over the last 19 years.

“Rethinking tomorrow’s communities now, builds our capacity to act with foresight and create resilient and liveable places”

Phillip Daffara

PRIORITY 7

Shift to Dynamic Planning and Green Infrastructure for Sustainable, Humane Settlements

A sustainable human settlement provides to its inhabitants not only the basic needs they require but also caters to higher level aspirations such as recreation, knowledge and cultural experiences. It has to be a self-sustaining community catering to all needs for all its citizens. For this, it is essential that every member of the community contribute to building up the kind of place they want to live in. Democratic participation, decentralisation, common property management and transparency are central to the development for such settlements.

Sustainable settlements are also about living in harmony with nature, fulfilling the needs of all inhabitants without destroying the natural resource base that sustains them. The design and management of future settlements will need to be much more sensitive to the resource implications of their operation. For example, new and innovative technological approaches such as permaculture and aquaponics offer opportunities for meeting demand while minimising resource consumption. In these times of rapid change, it is necessary that dynamic and systemic planning guidelines and processes set the rules of the game rather than prescribing rigid specifications for form and function. Needless to say, all players and the right size or scale of play have to be defined to avoid city growth from metastasising and possible collapse.

Settlements for the future need provision of adequate public transport systems coupled with appropriate zoning and planning for settlements taking into account current and projected growth. Enhanced mobility and connectivity, both virtual and physical for education and livelihoods, will enhance equity among inhabitants by creating equal opportunities for all, including pedestrians as much as motorists. A sustainable human settlement makes the lives of its citizens richer, builds social capital and regenerates natural capital while augmenting economic capital.

This development approach cannot be restricted to either urban or rural settings. Both urban and rural inhabitants need to be provided these facilities and amenities for holistic development. A sustainable human settlement, whether a smart city or village, needs smart citizens.

To create these sustainable human settlements India needs to:

- Re-evolve models of growth and development that contribute to regeneration of resource catchments for settlements
- Encourage youth and inhabitant engagement to play an active participatory role in the planning and operation of settlements
- Recast planning systems to develop systemic guidelines that enable dynamic and self-correcting settlement development
- Create a livelihood based approach to meeting the needs of the local population using locally available resources

impact

- 10 Humara Gaons in 2 States as models to influence government and inspire communities.
- Access of all to safe drinking water, housing and sanitation facilities for over 2,000 households
- Over half of total cultivated in 10 villages land brought under climate adaptive resource management
- Enterprise and community owned and managed service delivery models for basic needs established
- 100 green livelihoods and income generation acitivities adopted
- Informed and empowered community participation in local governance leading to improved right and entitlement access

Integrated village development for dynamic and self-sufficient settlements - Hamara Gaon

Uttar Pradesh and Madhya Pradesh, India

The current development strategies follow a siloed approach that fail to capitalise on the principle of the whole being more than the sum of its parts.

Development Alternatives has an integrated approach to village development – *Hamara Gaon* – an etymology that emphasises people's right to decide their development pathway as informed and empowered communities. The approach of the programme targets issues related to the economy, environment and society systemically, as a whole, helping communities realise the benefits of integrated development leading to the creating dynamic settlements characterised by self-propelled and sufficient economies

Embedded in holistic and sustainable thinking, the programme inspires ownership amongst the community, creates rational environmental management systems, promotes diversified and dynamic local economies and fosters social harmony. This is catalysed through creation of people-oriented institutions, dissemination of knowledge and appropriate technologies, strengthening local governance systems, and enabling access to credit and finance.

Hamara Gaon works on the principle of "Haryali, Udyamita aur Sampanata" – environment, economic, and social well being and prosperity. Capacities of local institutions are strengthened to plan and implement a range of integrated village development measures through accessing available government schemes. These include - integrated watershed management, infrastructure development such as roads, drains, housing, water supply, sanitation and electrification, literacy and livelihood initiatives, savings and credit services, farm and off farm enterprises identified on the basis of resource and market assessments and communication and information for change. The programme is led through local institutions and engagement with local government such that public schemes and development programmes can be leveraged. Wherever possible, the programme brings in investment from the community to instil sustainability, and creates partnerships with private sector for leveraging resources to amplify effectiveness.

impact

- More than twice the land is under irrigation than that of 1999
- Number of wells increased from 97 in 1991 to 284 in 2011
- Every villager lives in a pukka ghar (permanent structure)
- Per capita income rose from Rs. 830 in 1995 to Rs. 30,000 in 2012. In 2012, the village had 60 millionaires.

Photo Source: Mera Mukhiya (Blog)

Systemic and Integrated local planning for building humane settlements - Hiware Bazaar

Maharashtra, India

Hiware Bazar is a semi-arid village in Maharashtra that from the 1970s to the 1990s overused and depleted most of its natural endowments of water. The village faced an acute water crisis, during which only 12% of the land was cultivated, leading to declining agricultural productivity and rampant poverty in the region. Water retention was limited which further deteriorated by deforestation over the years. Available water was poorly managed, and access to water was determined by ownership of the land and capital to dig deeper and deeper wells.

The change took place in 1989, when the Panchayat, led by Popat Rao, engineered an integrated reform through the adoption of a decentralised model based on the needs of the people. To address the most pressing problem of water, the Panchayat, with support from the community, started a programme that channeled all the government drought compensation to create water conservation structures and reforest the area to restore the natural ecology. To prevent overuse of water in cultivation, energy and water-efficient technologies for irrigation, such as drip irrigation, were adopted in addition to watershed conservation techniques such as contour trenching and bunding, afforestation, building of earth embankments around hills and rain water harvesting.

The villagers were encouraged to consider water as a common pool resource and prioritise uses of available water. To institutionalise sharing of water, the village introduced a practice of water budgeting. Using a 'water bank' principle, the budgeting ensures that the village does not draw more water than it stores, and a small amount is kept in reserve. Depending on rainfall in the year, available water is allocated amongst various uses, with first priority for drinking water for humans. Of the remaining water, 70% is reserved for irrigation and 30% is stored for future use by allowing it to percolate and recharge groundwater.

The local communities were made the key stakeholders of the village. Responsibilities were divided amongst the residents who were organised into cooperative societies like the mutual interests groups, youth groups, SHG's and other forums. Livelihood programmes to utilise the natural resources in a productive manner were initiated. Regular meetings for collective decision making were organised for extensive and systemic involvement of the community. This democratic model of governance also empowered women and other marginalised sections of the society to come forward and participate in the process of development.

Today, with its outstanding natural, economic, social and physical capital base, Hiware Bazaar stands testimony to the fact that dynamic and sustainable planning can promote development of settlements as desired.

PRIORITY 8

Move from shareholder to stakeholder businesses

The traditional business model, in which the shareholder is the final decision making authority, focuses primarily on the company's strategy. This usually results in a business model with its foremost objective to increase the company's stock value, with relatively little concern for the interests of the other stakeholders (employees, suppliers, and customers).

In the course of transition to a sustainable economy, the business community will adopt a stakeholder oriented outlook and view the impact of business operations on a wide range of issues; including at least: profit, reputation, employees, supplies, customers, shareholders, the environment and the communities where the company conducts business. These businesses will no longer view value creation through the myopic lens of growth rate over short time but revise their bottom line to include social equity and environmental sustainability to create long term shared value for both businesses and society, not only as means to profit but also as ends.

The self-interest of business remains an important economic engine, but business interests, too, change. Enlightened businesses will increasingly seize the initiative, showing that eco-efficiency, green marketing and social responsibility offer a competitive advantage. Corporations should bear cost and responsibility of its operations and pursue new codes of conduct which are rewarded in the market place, while those that do not would be punished by an increasingly informed and vigilant public mobilised by the civil society. Big corporations and small business should both be important in this transition. .

For this, India should

- Encourage businesses to develop dynamic, resilient and inclusive business models and product lines geared to the needs of the poor
- Recruit and source locally and transfer knowledge and competence to local enterprises
- Provide support such as access to technology know-how, incentives, risk coverage, infrastructure for converting brown businesses to green ones that are profitable

"A business that makes nothing but money is a poor business" Henry Ford

Photo Credit: Last Forest Enterprise, Keystone Foundation

Business for the people and the planet - Last Forest Enterprise

Tamil Nadu, India

The Last Forest Enterprises is a green and inclusive marketing platform that sells a diverse range of value-added organic produce and forest products grown by local communities in the Nilgiri Biosphere Reserve. Incubated by Keystone Foundation, this social enterprise promotes fair-trade principles, economic development and environmentally benign practices for sustainable livelihoods that promote triple bottom line wellbeing.

Traditionally, indigenous communities sold their goods in neighbouring areas or to middlemen, at negligible prices. To enable the communities to attain higher returns, Last Forest integrated with such smallholder producers, farmers, forest-dwellers and the indigenous community. The enterprise checks quality, packages and markets locally produced under-valued commodities to mainstream green and responsible consumption.

Products like handicrafts, garments, spices, honey and timber products are procured at a markup price, quality-checked and branded by the enterprise from eight production clusters and sold at three enterprise-operated retail shops, marketed and sold on e-commerce portals, and supplied to retail dealers across the country. Moreover, the enterprise continually engages with the local communities to build their capacities for value addition with new age technologies. Through its model, Last Forest Enterprises incentivises the communities to grow and harvest organically and sustainably by offering better prices and making available health insurance and other benefits. The steady earnings strengthen the pride and dignity and enables families to invest in health and education. Besides the personal incomes, a portion of the business profit is relayed back to the community for education, infrastructure and village development.

At present, Last Forest is working with 60 producer groups across the country. This initiative emphasises fair trade, sustainable harvesting and integration with local communities. As a platform that promotes these principles, Last Forest paves a path for a sustainable development for all.

impact

- 800 enterprises created
- 1.1 million metric tonnes soil saved
- 700,000 metric tonnes waste utlised
- 130,000 metric tonnes carbon emissions saved

Technology based business models for green and inclusive growth – TARA Machines and Tech Services Pvt. Ltd, *India*

TARA Machines and Tech Services Pvt. Ltd. – an affiliate of Development Alternatives - is a part of a new breed of enterprises that have a stakeholder oriented business model, collectively termed social enterprises. The company has developed small business packages based on green building material production technologies. These innovative technologies provide 'Waste to Wealth' business solutions for an expanding network of enterprises in the SME sector in India. The TARA Machines product range is unique and developed for the Indian market place to cater specifically to small-scale enterprises. Through these enterprises, affordable building products for construction have been made available in rural India.

TARA Machines provides total a business solution to enable its entrepreneur maximise profitability and minimise risk. As a result, it has a strong focus on technical support, material and product testing, training and regular servicing along with machinery. It creates profitable enterprises across the country that convert industrial waste into building material like roofing tiles, floor tiles and pavers, fly ash bricks and blocks, to be able to service customers at affordable costs and support the construction of eco-friendly houses in rural and peri-urban regions in a decentralised model.

The TARA Machines business model is both fundamentally green and inclusive. The technologies it has introduced to the market use waste as a primary input material, instead of virgin natural materials such as soil, coal and wood. Waste created on an industrial scale, such as fly ash from thermal power stations, are recycled to create material. As the primary input is waste, the building material also becomes affordable. Every enterprise set up by TARA Machines contributes significantly to the employment and development of the local economy. By setting up local enterprises, the TARA Machines business model ensures every enterprise acts as a multiplier for both environmental and social benefit, creating true triple bottom line impact.

"Building…a sustainable future … will need open dialogue among all branches of national, regional and local government….And it will need the engagement of all stakeholders - including the private sector and civil society, and especially the poor and marginalised"

Ban Ki-moon

PRIORITY 9

Strengthen Local Government and Civil Society Cooperation for Community Empowerment

None of the conventional sectors could, in their present form, answer the Central Question stated at the beginning: How do we build a sustainable future for India? Each is one busy solving their problems, creating their own conceptual and operational frameworks, and dedicated to their own continued existence.

For development to be sustainable, the people of India must acquire a sense of ownership and responsibility for their resources — economic, social and natural. They must be able to oversee and correct the actions of their elected representatives on a continuing basis. They must be vigilant and prevent or stop activities that are against the interest of the community, particularly its environment. Such a sense of ownership can in the long run come only from actual ownership — enshrined in institutions of local governance involving the entire adult population.

However, bringing about widespread change requires the concerted efforts of everyone in a position to influence social and behavioural change. Since such a change has not been achieved by governments and businesses so far, the civil society (which includes most organisations that are not in the government or private sectors) must provide the leadership for this. Although civil society hasn't, so far, fared much better in delivering the results needed than either government or business, it could serve as a key catalyst and source, if it evolves its sense of professionalism, independence and responsibility, of new institutional designs for building a better and more equitable world.

By providing strong leadership, civil society could, in principle, position itself even to influence the practices of the public and private sectors. It can bring in knowledge from grassroots to bear upon policy development. It can help test and validate transformative innovations on ground by reaching out and building capacities of communities for adopting mass behaviour change and public accountability. Civil society organisations could work from the bottom up to address poverty from the perspective of the poor themselves. They can channel resources back to the livelihood economy through collective institutions, financial systems and appropriate technology and foster cooperation among businesses, governments and communities.

To facilitate such community empowerment India needs to:

- Devolve substantial independence in revenue and expenditure and increased autonomy to local bodies for designing, implementing, coordinating, and monitoring programmes
- Strengthen capabilities of local bodies to assess local priorities and needs through proactive engagement with community members
- Engage CSOs in proactive decision-making processes of the government

impact

- A network of 650 CSOs strengthened
- 40,000 CBOs formed in the project areas over half of which are women's self-help groups
- 600,000 people access entitlements amounting to a monthly incremental addition of Rs.270 plus on an average

Strengthening Civil Society for sustainable social impact - Poorest Areas Civil Society (PACS) Programme

Bihar, Uttar Pradesh, Madhya Pradesh, Chhatisgarh, Jharkhand and Maharashtra, India

PACS was initiated as a comprehensive civil society response programme to promote civil society led development action in 108 of the poorest districts in the six states. The initiative adopted a unique strategy for multiplier and sustainable development impact by building capacities of civil society to become local agents of change. With a focus to enable poor people to realise their entitlements, the programme has been successful in reaching out to 40.4 million poor people in the poorest areas in about 20,000 villages in partnership with 650 CSOs. More than 80 per cent of the population covered by the programme was from scheduled castes, scheduled tribes and backward classes, and the remaining proportion from the general class was also economically vulnerable.

The strategic and integrated approach followed in PACS included awareness generation and grassroots advocacy with local government institutions for empowering women, reducing social exclusion, and generating livelihood opportunities for the poor. The programme led to communities accessing increased entitlements and improved local implementation of development programmes like midday meal scheme in schools; regular attendance of schoolteachers and health workers; greater participation in gram sabha meeting and recognition of community strength by officials and policymakers.

PACS was funded by the UK Government's Department for International Development (DFID) and managed by Development Alternatives.

Photo Credit: Social Cops

Driving transparency and accountability in governance systems - Wada Na Todo Abhiyaan, Social Cops, *India*

Civil society organisations in recent times have encouraged accountability and informed decision-making processes of the government. While there are many avenues for citizens to influence their governance, the Wada Na Todo Abhiyan and Social Cops are two initiatives that represent two distinct approaches to enable such participatory governance and accountability.

Wada Na Todo Abhiyan is a national campaign to hold the government accountable for its promise to end Poverty, Social Exclusion & Discrimination. It emerged from the consensus among human rights activists and social action groups who were part of the World Social Forum 2004 to create an environment through focused and concerted effort and try to make a difference in India where one-fourth of the world's poor exist and they continuously experience intense deprivation from opportunities to learn, live and work in dignity. The Wada Na Todo Abhiyan aims to hold the government accountable to its promises. It monitors the commitments made by the government to meet the objectives set in the UN Millennium Declaration, the National Development Goals and the National Common Minimum Program with a special focus on the Right to Livelihood, Health & Education. Through its initiatives and campaigns, Wada Na Todo Abhiyan has been able to bring together more than 4,000 rights action groups across 23 states of India through its activities and initiatives.

Social Cops is a technology company on a mission to solve the world's most pressing problems using data. Using its platform and solutions, Social Cops works across with non-profits and governments to build capacity for data collection, analysis and visualisation. It aims to advocate evidence-based action by tracking and monitoring important parameters of development programmes. By using a combination of online information extraction, open data and mobile applications to collect data, the platform processes millions of discrete data points to provide meaningful information. These insights are aimed to empower key decision-makers such as governments, corporate heads, policymakers, non-profits and media houses to make decisions driven by data. The Social Cops data station available on the website allows people to peruse data relevant to them on a variety of topics of general interest.

The Wada Na Todo Abhiyan and Social Cops, though different in their method of functioning, both provide excellent examples of how civil society can influence decisions that affect them, oversee the actions of their elected representatives and facilitate a more democratic and equitable existence for all.

MOVING FORWARD ...

Transiting to a greener, more equitable economy and society is not going to be easy nor simple. With having chosen the path, strategic levers of change will need to be identified such that we are able to manage the trade-offs and convert them into synergies.

Transiting to a greener, more equitable economy and society will not be either easy or without resistance from those whose stakes are in the present system. Given the alternative, of a following a so-called "development" path leading to a dead-end for both modern civilisation and for much of our life-support systems, we do not have much choice but to pursue this transition with vigour. Strategic levers of change will need to be identified such that we are able to manage the trade-offs and convert them into synergies. Key game changers for a more sustainable future are - women who are truly empowered, workers with appropriate skills, youth with leadership qualities, adequately supported micro and small industries, an independent and active civil society, full cost accounting systems for all investments along with institutions of governance committed to universality and sustainability A whole new approach is now needed that goes beyond the shibboleths and dichotomies of the past needs to be adopted for a sustainable India. The future of India will be built on the basis of decisions we take today, on the values we ascribe to all life and nature, on our shared understanding of the definition of development and modernity and on the indicators we use to measure our progress. The institutions we form and nurture, the technologies we choose, the economic instruments we use, and the governance frame we accept will change it and make it - **The future is ours to choose and make.**

EndNotes

1. *Panchsheel* has originated from Sanskrit, meaning 'five virtues' (panch: five, sheel: virtues)
2. Minhas, S., 1970, *'Rural Poverty, Land Redistribution And Development Strategy: Facts And Policy, Indian Economic Review New Series'*, Vol. 5, No. 1, pp. 97-128
3. Planning Commission, 2013, *'Poverty Estimates For 2011-2012'*, Government of India
4. Forbes Billionaire List, 2015
5. Census of India, 2011
6. World Bank Database (last updated 2015)
7. World Bank Database (last updated 2015)
8. Minhas, S., 1970, *'Rural Poverty, Land Redistribution And Development Strategy: Facts And Policy, Indian Economic Review New Series',* Vol. 5, No. 1, pp. 97-128
9. Planning Commission, 2013, *'Poverty Estimates For 2011-2012'*, Government of India
10. World Bank Group, 2013, *'India Development Update'*
11. Social Progress Index, The Social Imperative 2014 (http://www.socialprogressimperative.org)
12. Human Development Report, United Nations Development Programme 2014
13. Planning Commission, 2013, *'Poverty Estimates For 2011-2012'*, Government of India
14. Planning Commission, 2013, *'Poverty Estimates For 2011-2012'*, Government of India
15. National Commission for Enterprises in the Unorganised Sector, 2007, *'Report on Conditions of Work and Promotion of Livelihoods in the Unorganised Sector'*
16. Todhunter, C., 2014, *'The Global Multidimensional Poverty Index: Rising Poverty and Social Inequality in India'*
17. Gupta, R., Sankhe, S., & Dobbs, R., 2014, *'From Poverty To Empowerment: India's Imperative For Jobs, Growth, And Effective Basic Services'*, McKinsey Global Institute
18. Economic Survey of India 2012-13
19. Rao, G. R. S., 2005, *'Gross Social Conflict- Towards A Framework Of Analysis, Measurement And Management'*
20. The Economist, 2014 *'The Future of Jobs'*. Available from: <http://www.economist.com/news/briefing/21594264-previous-technological-innovation-has-always-delivered-more-long-run-employment-not-less>
21. Institute of Applied Manpower Research, Planning Commission, 2012, *'Joblessness and Informalization: Challenges to Inclusive Growth in India'*
22. Institute of Applied Manpower Research, Planning Commission, 2012, *'Joblessness and Informalization: Challenges to Inclusive Growth in India'*
23. 68th Round of the National Sample Survey, 2011-12
24. Chandrashekhar, C.P. (2014) as quoted in the Hindu and the Business Line
25. Institute of Applied Manpower Research, Planning Commission, 2012, *'Joblessness and Informalization: Challenges to Inclusive Growth in India'*
26. Binswanger-Mkhize, H P, 2013, *'The Stunted Structural Transformation of the Indian Economy',* Economic and Political Weekly
27. Asian Development Bank, 2012, *'Confronting Inequality in Asia',* Asian Development Outlook
28. Ravindranath (N. H.) et al., 2014, *'Forest area estimation and reporting: implications for conservation, management and REDD+'*, Current Science, Volume 106, Number 9
29. Forest Survey of India, 2013
30. Ministry of Environment and Forests, 2014, *'Desertification, Land Degradation and Drought in Context of India'*
31. Asian Development Bank Institute, 2012, *'Asia's Wicked Environmental Problems'*
32. Global Footprint Network, 2010, *'The Ecological Wealth Of Nations'*
33. Indo-German Environment Group, 2013, *'India's Future Needs for Resources: Dimensions, Challenges and Possible Solutions'*
34. United Nations, Department of Economic and Social Affairs, Population Division, 2014, *'World Urbanisation Prospects: The 2014 Revision'*
35. Blue solutions is derived from the concept of blue economy by Gunter Pauli (President of ZERI and a Senior Advisor to Development Alternatives), which gives priority to local systems of production and consumption as the major means to improve the human condition and maintain the environmental resource base.

Further Readings

Alkire S. and Seth S., 2013, *'Multidimensional Poverty Reduction in India 1999-2006: Slower Progress for the Poorest Groups'*, Oxford Poverty and Human Development Initiative

Anand, M. C., Chopra, V., & Niazi, Z., 2012, *'Understanding Rural Habitat: Lessons in Sustainablity,* Development Alternatives

Banerjee, A. V., & Duflo, E., 2003, *'Inequality And Growth: What Can The Data Say?',* Journal of Economic Growth

Bauer, S. et al, 2012, *'Unlocking Business Dynamism To Promote Green (Sustainable And Inclusive) Growth: Learning From Innovation In Emerging Economies'*, Available from <http://www.odi.org.uk>

Bergh, G., & Melamed, C., 2012, *'Inclusive Growth And A Post-2015 Framework'*, Overseas Development Institute

Bhagwati, J., & Panagariya, A., 2013, '*Why Growth Matters: How Economic Growth in India Reduced Poverty and the Lessons for Other Developing Countries'*

Bhagwati, J., 1993, '*India In Transition: Freeing The Economy*', OUP Catalogue.

Bhattacharya, 2013, *'Everything You Wanted To Know About The Sen-Bhagwati Debate'*, Live Mint 20 July <http://www.livemint.com/Politics>

Binswanger-Mkhize H.P., 2013, *'The Stunted Structural Transformation Of The Indian Economy: Agriculture, Manufacturing And The Rural Non-Farm Sector'*, Economic and Political Weekly, Vol. xlvill Nos 26 & 27

Brock, H., 2011, '*Competition Over Resources: Drivers Of Insecurity And The Global South*' Oxford Research Group, September, Available from <http://www.oxfordresearchgroup.org.uk>

Bundestag, D., 2011, '*Towards Green Growth: Monitoring Progress*'.

Chang, H. J., 2002, '*Kicking Away The Ladder: Development Strategy In Historical Perspective*', Anthem Press

Chang, H. J., 2009, *'Hamlet without the Prince of Denmark: How development has disappeared from today's 'development' discourse'*, University of Cambridge

Cobham, A., & Sumner, A., 2013, '*Is It All About The Tails? The Palma Measure Of Income Inequality*', Center for Global Development, Working Paper

Cornia, G. A., & Court, J., 2004, '*Inequality, Growth, And Poverty In An Era Of Liberalization And Globalization*', Oxford University Press Oxford

Cornia, G. A., 2003, '*The Impact Of Liberalisation And Globalisation On Income Inequality In Developing And Transitional Economies*', CESifo, Working Paper

Costanza R., Hart M., Posner S., & Talberth J., 2009, '*Beyond GDP: The Need For New Measures Of Progress',* Pardee Papers, No. 4

Deloitte and All India Management Association, 2011, '*Inclusive Growth: A Challenging Opportunity'*

Development Alternatives & World Resource Institute, 2014, *'A Transformative Post-2015 Development Agenda'*, Independent Research Forum

Development Alternatives & Wuppertal Institute, 2014, '*Decoupling Growth From Resource Consumption'*

Development Alternatives & Wuppertal Institute, 2014, '*Policy Perspective – A Framework: Decoupling Growth from Natural Recourses'*

Development Alternatives, 2011, '*Low Carbon Pathways: Farmers Adaptation Cluster'*

Development Alternatives, 2011, *'Low Carbon Pathways: Sustainable Civil Society Initiatives to Address Global Environmental Challenges'*

Drèze, J., & Sen, A., 2013, '*An Uncertain Glory: India And Its Contradictions*', Princeton University Press.

Drèze, J., 2006, '*National Employment Guarantee Inaction',* The Hindu, 12 September, Available from: <http://www.thehindu.com>

Economic and Political Weekly, 2014, '*Overcoming Sub-5% Growth, Economic and Political Weekly',* Editorial, Vol. xlix No 28

Ellen Macarthur Foundation and McKinsey and Company, 2014, '*Towards The Circular Economy: Accelerating The Scale-Up Across Global Supply Chains'*

Ellen Macarthur Foundation, 2013, '*Towards The Circular Economy: Opportunities For The Consumer Goods Sector, Rethink The Future'*

Ernst von Weizsaecker, 2009, *Factor Five: Transforming the Global Economy through 80% Improvements in Resource Productivity*

Fukuda-Parr, S., 2003, '*The Human Development Paradigm: Operationalizing Sen's Ideas On Capabilities',* Feminist Economics

Galor, O., 2009, '*Inequality And Economic Development: An Overview*', Providence, RI: Brown University.

Ghose, A. K., 2001, *'Global Economic Inequality And International Trade'*, International Labour Office, Employment Sector

Ghosh J., 2002, '*Social Policy In Indian Development*', Prepared for the UNRISD project on Social Policy in a Development Context

Ghosh, J. 2012, '*Redefining Development And Quality Of Life: New Economic Strategies In Ecuador*', Economic and Political Weekly, Vol. xlvil No. 7

Growth, P. P., 2006, '*Infrastructure'*, OECD, Available from: <http://www.poverty-wellbeing.net>

Guha, R., 2007, '*India After Gandhi: The History Of The World's Largest Democracy*'

Haan, A., 2013, *The Social Policies Of Emerging Economies: Growth And Welfare In China And India*, International Development Research Centre (IDRC), Working Paper No. 110

Hammond A.L. et al, 2007, *The Next 4 Billion: Market Size And Business Strategy At The Base Of The Pyramid*, World Resource Institute and International Finance Corporation

Harris J., 2000, '*Basic Principles Of Sustainable Development, Global Development And Environment Institute'*, Working Paper No. 00-04

Heintz J., 2009, '*Employment, Economic Development, And Poverty Reduction: Critical Issues And Policy Challenges*', Commissioned for the UNRISD Flagship Report on Poverty Project on Poverty Reduction and Policy Regimes

Himanshu & Sen A., 2013, '*In-Kind Food Transfers – I: Impact On Poverty'*, Economic and Political Weekly, Vol. xlvill Nos. 45 & 46

Himanshu and Sen A., 2013, '*In-Kind Food Transfers – II: Impact On Nutrition And Implications For Food Security And Its Costs'*, Economic and Political Weekly, Vol. xlvill No. 47

Jackson, T., & Victor, P. A., 2013, '*Green EconomyAt Community Scale'*, Metcalf Foundation

Jacobs, M., 2012, '*Green Growth: Economic Theory And Political Discourse*', Grantham Research Institute on Climate Change and the Environment, Working Paper

Jones, H., Higgins, K., & Bird, K., 2009, '*Equity In Development: Why It Is Important And How To Achieve It*', Overseas Development Institute

Kapila, U., 2009, '*Indian Economy Since Independence*', Academic Foundation

Khan, M. H., 2008, '*Governance, Growth and Development'*, Commissioned for the UNRISD Flagship Report on Poverty Project on Poverty Reduction and Policy Regimes

Khosla, A., 2008, '*Leveraging Knowledge to End Poverty*', Global Development

Khosla, A., 2013, '*Beyond Rio: From Green Economy To Green Society*', Economy of Sufficiency

King, M., 2013, '*Green Growth And Poverty Reduction*', OECD Development Co-operation, Working Papers No. 14

Kothari, A., 2013, *'Development And Ecological Sustainability In India: Possibilities For The Post-2015 Framework',* Global Development Network

Kundu A. & Saraswati L.R., 2012, '*Migration And Exclusionary Urbanisation In India*', Economic and Political Weekly, Vol. xlvii Nos. 26 & 27

Kundu A., 2011, '*Politics And Economics Of Urban Growth*', Economic and Political Weekly, Vol. xlvI No. 20

Kundu A., Pradhan B.K, & Subramanian A., 2002, '*Dichotomy Or Continuum: Analysis Of Impact Of Urban Centres On Their Periphery*', Economic and Political Weekly

McKay, A. (n.d.), '*Inequality Briefing*', Overseas Development Institute, Available from <http://www.gsdrc.org/docs/open/SE4.pdf>

McKinsey Global Institute, 2014, *'From Poverty To Empowerment: India's Imperative For Jobs, Growth, And Effective Basic Services'*

Meadows, D., 2008, '*Thinking In Systems'*

Mehrotra S., 2012, '*Joblessness And Informalization: Challenges To Inclusive Growth In India*', Institute of Applied Manpower Research, Planning Commission, Government of India

Nayyar, D., 1998, '*Economic Development And Political Democracy: Interaction Of Economics And Politics In Independent India,* Economic and Political Weekly

Nayyar, D., 2006, '*Economic Growth in Independent India Lumbering Elephant or Running Tiger?',* Economic and Political Weekly

Niazi, Z., & Thakur, M., 2014, '*Equity Issues In A Green Economy'*, Development Alternatives

OECD, 2012, '*Equity and Quality in Education',* OECD Publishing, Available from: <http://www.oecd-ilibrary.org>

OECD, 2013, '*Economic Policy Reforms',* OECD Publishing, Available from: <http://www.oecd-ilibrary.org>

Outcome Document Rio+20, '*The Future We Want'*

Pauli, G., 2010, '*The Blue Economy: 10 Years, 100 Innovations, 100*

Million Jobs'

Pauli G. 2015, *'The Blue Economy Version 2.0 200 Projects Implemented US $ 4 Billion Invested 3 Million Jobs Created'*

Perch, L., Watson, C., & Barry, B. 2012, *'Resource Inequality: Moving Inequalities From The Periphery To The Centre Of The Post-2015 Agenda',* United Nations Development Programme

Platform, G. G. K., 2013, *'Moving Towards A Common Approach On Green Growth Indicators',* Available from: <http://www.unep.org/greeneconomy>

Raskin, P. D., 2006, *'World Lines: Pathways, Pivots, and the Global Future'*

Raskin, P., 2006, '*The Great Transition Today: A Report From The Future*', Boston MA: Tellus Institute

Raskin, P., et al, 2002, '*Great Transition: The Promise And Lure Of The Times Ahead*', Estocolmo: Stockholm Environment Institute

Sachs, J. D., & Someshwar, S., 2012, '*Green Growth And Equity In The Context Of Climate Change: Some Considerations*', East Asian Bureau of Economic Research

Sankhe, S., Vittal, I., & Dobbs, R., 2010, *'India's Urban Awakening: Building Inclusive Cities Sustaining Economic Growth'*, McKinsey Global Institute

Sen, A., 1999, *'Development As Freedom',* Oxford University Press

Sengupta, A., 2000, '*Realizing The Right To Development*', Development and Change

Sengupta, A., Kannan, K. P., & Raveendran, G., 2008, *'India's Common People: Who Are They, How Many Are They And How Do They Live?*', Economic and Political Weekly

Sharma, K., 2008, *'PACS NREGA Campaign Report 2008',* Development Alternatives

Shell Scenarios, 2012, <http://www.shell.com/global/future-energy/scenarios.html>

Solomon, K. R. et al, 1996. *Ecological Risk Assessment Of Atrazine In North American Surface Waters,* Environmental Toxicology and Chemistry

South Asia Co-operative Environment Programme, 2014, *'Post 2015 South Asia Development Agenda'*

Studies, D. U., 1980, *'Bangladesh'* Available from: <http://ilo.ch/wcmsp5/groups/public/---dgreports/---dcomm/documents/publication/wcms_229105.pdf>

Thorbecke, E., & Charumilind, C., 2002, *'Economic Inequality And Its Socioeconomic Impact,* World Development

UNEP-International Resource Panel, 2011, *'Decoupling Natural Resource Use And Environmental Impacts From Economic Growth'*

UNEP-International Resource Panel, 2013, *'Mainstreaming Resource Management Concerns in Human Well-being Goals',* Development Alternatives

UNEP-International Resource Panel, 2013, *'Managing and Conserving The Natural Resource Base For Sustained Economic and Social Development',* Development Alternatives

UNEP, 2011, *'Towards A Green Economy: Pathways To Sustainable Development And Poverty Eradication - A Synthesis For Policy Makers*', www.unep.org/greeneconomy

UNEP, 2012, *'Sustainable Consumption and Production and Poverty Alleviation'*

United Nations Inter-Agency Task Force on Social and Solidarity Economy (TFSSE), n.d., *'Social And Solidarity Economy And The Challenge Of Sustainable Development'*

Utting P., Dijk N., & Matheï M.A., 2014, *'Social And Solidarity Economy: Is There A New Economy In The Making?*', Occasional Paper 10, Potential and Limits of Social and Solidarity Economy, United Nations Research Institute for Social Development

Vandemoortele M., 2013, *'Building Blocks For Equitable Growth: Lessons From The BRICS*, Overseas Development Institute, Working Paper 365

World Bank, 2012, *'Inclusive Green Growth: The Pathway To Sustainable Development*', The World Bank, Available from: <http://elibrary.worldbank.org/doi/book/10.1596/978-0-8213-9551-6>

World Economic Forum, 2005, *'India And The World: Scenarios To 2025'*

Websites referred for Case Studies

www.hiware-bazar.epanchayat.in
www.ifad.org
www.inhabitat.com
www.instituciones.sld.cu/elam
www.lastforest.in
www.socialcops.org
www.villgro.org
www.wadanatodo.net
www.zed.in
www. zeri.org